GAZING AT STARS

Stories from Asia

These stories come from India, Malaysia, Singapore, and China – different countries, different cultures, but the universal thread of family relationships runs through them all. A husband still feels the pain of a failed marriage, a new young wife finds a world she doesn't like, and a mother is bitterly disappointed in her daughter. Other stories give us a grandmother aching with love for her young granddaughter, a father being punished for his wrongdoing, a family arguing over money – an argument familiar the world over. There are also stories about children: Anil, who sees what he ought not to have seen, and Manju, who watches with the pitiless clear sight of a child as her older brother – in the words of Gilbert Koh's poem – gazes at stars, stumbles, trips, and falls painfully in love.

BOOKWORMS WORLD STORIES

English has become an international language, and is used on every continent, in many varieties, for all kinds of purposes. *Bookworms World Stories* are the latest addition to the Oxford Bookworms Library. Their aim is to bring the best of the world's stories to the English language learner, and to celebrate the use of English for storytelling all around the world.

Jennifer Bassett
Series Editor

Accident

And I,
gazing at stars,
stumbled over you,
tripped
and
fell painfully in love,
couldn't get up
for ages.

Gilbert Koh (1973–)
a lawyer working in Singapore, winner of
the 2005 Golden Point Award for Poetry

OXFORD BOOKWORMS LIBRARY
World Stories

Gazing at Stars

Stories from Asia

Stage 6 (2500 headwords)

Series Editor: Jennifer Bassett
Founder Editor: Tricia Hedge
Activities Editors: Jennifer Bassett and Christine Lindop

NOTES ON THE ILLUSTRATORS

KIM SENG (illustrations on pages 5, 79, 101) was born in Vietnam, and is half Chinese, half Cambodian. He arrived in New Zealand as a refugee at the age of four, and now lives in Wellington, where he studied illustration at Massey University. He is passionate about using illustrations to convey stories and ideas.

CHANDRAMOHAN KULKARNI (illustrations on pages 14, 61, 91) was born in 1956 in Pune, Maharashtra, India. He has been a freelance artist for many years, working in book illustration and cover design. He has done almost 5,000 cover designs, and illustrates contemporary literature in Marathi, a local Indian language. His work is shown in exhibitions throughout India.

ZID (illustrations on pages 28, 50), a Malaysian now living in Singapore, was born in 1983. His full name is Mohammad Yazid Kamal Baharin, and he works as a freelance painter, illustrator, and comic artist in both real and digital media. He has done several art shows.

RETOLD BY CLARE WEST

Gazing at Stars

Stories from Asia

OXFORD UNIVERSITY PRESS

OXFORD
UNIVERSITY PRESS

Great Clarendon Street, Oxford OX2 6DP

Oxford University Press is a department of the University of Oxford.
It furthers the University's objective of excellence in research, scholarship,
and education by publishing worldwide in

Oxford New York

Auckland Cape Town Dar es Salaam Hong Kong Karachi
Kuala Lumpur Madrid Melbourne Mexico City Nairobi
New Delhi Shanghai Taipei Toronto

With offices in

Argentina Austria Brazil Chile Czech Republic France Greece
Guatemala Hungary Italy Japan Poland Portugal Singapore
South Korea Switzerland Thailand Turkey Ukraine Vietnam

OXFORD and OXFORD ENGLISH are registered trade marks of
Oxford University Press in the UK and in certain other countries

ISBN: 978 0 19 479420 6

A complete recording of this Bookworms edition of
Gazing at Stars: Stories from Asia is available in an audio CD pack. ISBN: 978 0 19 479419 0

Printed in China

Word count (main text): 28,539

For more information on the Oxford Bookworms Library,
visit www.oup.com/elt/bookworms

ACKNOWLEDGEMENTS

The publishers are grateful to the following for permission to adapt and simplify copyright texts:
to the author for *My Beloved Charioteer* from *Collected Stories Vol I* (Penguin Books India, 2003) by
Shashi Deshpande; to Liu Hong for *Taken for a Ride* broadcast on BBC Radio 4, 21 November 2007;
to Shama Habibullah and Waris Hussein for *The First Party* by their late mother Attia Hosain (first
published in *Phoenix Fled*, Chatto and Windus, 1953); to Noraishah Ismail for *Lily*; to Catherine Lim
for *Family*; to Ridjal Noor for *Anil*; to Preeta Samarasan for *Fair Trade*; to Nirupama Subramanian for
A Child is Born; to Hwee Hwee Tan for *Mid-Autumn*; to Ovidia Yu for *A Dream of China*

CONTENTS

INTRODUCTION   i
NOTES ON THE ILLUSTRATORS   iv
ACKNOWLEDGEMENTS   vi
NOTE ON THE LANGUAGE   viii

CHINA
Taken for a Ride   *Liu Hong*   1

INDIA
The First Party   *Attia Hosain*   9

MALAYSIA
Fair Trade   *Preeta Samarasan*   16

SINGAPORE
Mid-Autumn   *Hwee Hwee Tan*   36

MALAYSIA
Anil   *Ridjal Noor*   47

INDIA
My Beloved Charioteer   *Shashi Deshpande* 57

SINGAPORE
A Dream of China   *Ovidia Yu*   68

MALAYSIA
Lily   *Nora Adam*   82

INDIA
A Child is Born   *Nirupama Subramanian*   89

SINGAPORE
Family   *Catherine Lim*   92

GLOSSARY   105
ACTIVITIES: Before Reading   108
ACTIVITIES: After Reading   109
ABOUT THE AUTHORS   113
ABOUT THE BOOKWORMS LIBRARY   117

NOTE ON THE LANGUAGE

There are many varieties of English spoken in the world, and the characters in these stories from different Asian countries sometimes use non-standard forms (for example, leaving out auxiliary verbs such as *are* and *is*, leaving out the article *the*, and so on). There are also differences in word order, and some words which are used in different ways, such as *also*. This is how the authors of the original stories represented the spoken language that their characters would actually use in real life.

There are also words that are usually only found in Asian varieties of English (for example, *mooncake*), and a few words from Asian languages (for example, *gfi sim*).

All these words are either explained in the stories or in the glossary on page 105.

Taken for a Ride

LIU HONG

A story from China, retold by Clare West

In China, as in every country, traditions change over the years. In an old wedding ceremony the married couple were carried in a sedan chair, to the sound of a trumpet playing and songs about love and harmony and good fortune.

Jinnan runs his own wedding chair business, for couples who like the old customs, but his heart is heavy as he sings the familiar songs, remembering his own wife Lili . . .

'In this fortunate hour of extreme happiness, the newly married are seated . . .' Jinnan sang out in a loud but beautifully accented voice. This was his first day back at work after his wife Lili had left him, and he was glad that he was managing to sound calm, even joyful, for the occasion. He was surprised by the reflection of his wide smile in the shining *Suernai* trumpet as he raised it to his mouth and blew a short sharp burst on it. At this signal the four sedan carriers, all dressed in soft blue silk, their cheeks painted red, picked up the poles at the four corners, lifted the chair on to their shoulders, and waited for Jinnan's orders.

'Let the journey begin!' Jinnan called, and blew once more on the *Suernai* – a lively, joyous note. The late morning sun beat down on the procession, on the sedan covered with red silk and flowers, and on the four carriers, whose cheeks grew redder as they walked. Their bodies rocked from side to side, as they balanced the weight of the couple in the sedan. Jinnan led the procession, his waist moving this way and that as he blew the trumpet – in spite of his heavy heart, his body could not resist the music he had known since childhood. As he wiped the sweat from his face, he saw, through the thin curtain at the sedan window, the bride's gloved hands covering her face as her shoulders moved up and down. It was an odd thing to do. The woman had been veiled when she got into the sedan, and now Jinnan could not tell if she was laughing or crying. He looked in at the couple more closely, but the bride continued to bury her face in her hands as if she had something to hide.

These days, the ride in the sedan chair was no longer considered a necessary part of a wedding. Young people now just saw it as a pleasant way of reminding them of the traditions of the old days. Over the years Jinnan had witnessed many emotions in the couples who had taken the ride – delight, contentment, confusion, wonder. But somehow he found this particular couple disturbing. To start with, there was hardly any sound coming from inside the sedan, and when something *was* heard, it was always the groom speaking, in his heavy southern accent. The bride gave soft, short answers. Had they had an argument, on this of all days? Despite his own misery, Jinnan still wanted his customers to be happy.

The procession passed through a narrow street lined with restaurants and cafés. Next to the bright new Sea Food Heaven restaurant lay a large area of new building, where most of the construction workers were too busy to look at the passing sedan. Only one man paused to look down, and for a moment Jinnan seemed to catch sight of his former self. Not so long ago, he had been a construction worker just like those men – one of the city's low-paid slaves. He was lucky to have got out of it after a couple of years. The sedan ride was one of many wedding traditions that were becoming fashionable again, and that meant he could find a job as a *Suernai* trumpeter. Soon afterwards he was able to start his own wedding sedan service, employing four friends from his village to help him. The job suited him well. Blowing his trumpet and dancing along with the eyes of the crowd on him, he felt he was where he belonged.

The carriers were walking faster now. They had become used to the weight, and knew they were over halfway to their destination.

'Like jewels that connect, and jade that matches, may your married life be harmonious,' Jinnan sang.

His men joined in with their deep voices, 'Life is sweet. Two birds that fly side by side, two flowers that grow on the same plant . . .'

Suddenly Jinnan was full of sadness, remembering the way these same words had moved Lili. When he first met her, she was selling clothes in a market. She had seen him giving his performance and had fallen in love with him.

'I could tell you meant everything you said,' she said. City boys were not sincere, she had told him, they wanted fun, not marriage. She was looking for someone who would stay with her for ever, someone she could 'grow white hair' with. It was she who had encouraged him to start his own wedding chair business.

Jinnan shook his body more wildly, as if to throw off the memory of Lili. Losing himself in the performance, he raised the *Suernai* with his right hand and blew it as hard as he could. He didn't even know the name of the tune he was playing; it was simply something his grandfather and his own father had played for years at villagers' weddings in the countryside.

They had arrived at the bridge, where a large crowd had gathered to watch what they knew would be the highlight of the procession. He put the trumpet down and took a deep breath. Then he turned to face the sedan.

'In peace and harmony,' he said, 'a ride to the pleasure of love. She the instrument and he the player.'

'Music in harmony, music in harmony,' repeated the men.

At his command, the four carriers started to move the sedan playfully up and down; their singing grew faster and more breathless. The crowd came closer, expecting to hear the screams of the bride, pretending to be frightened, and the deep voice of the groom, calming her down. As Jinnan danced for his audience's amusement, he deliberately moved away from the sedan – the couple's cries of joy and pleasure would have brought back unbearable memories of being in the sedan with Lili. That day, on their own wedding ride, Lili, who sat with her body tightly against his, had worn a traditional red wedding dress, and her smiling face had looked like the most beautiful flower he had ever seen. But this time the crowd were disappointed. However hard they tried, they could hear no sound from inside the sedan.

Jinnan approached the chair again, and through its curtain he saw, written inside in red, 'Double Happiness' – a special celebratory word for weddings. The bride's head was still bent low as if in deep thought, half-covered by her hands. Why was she not looking at her husband? Were they still arguing? Jinnan turned to face the crowd, and went on with his speech.

'Be a dutiful son and daughter; may you produce a fat little boy or girl, and may your family do well!'

*The bride's head was still bent low as if in deep thought,
half-covered by her hands.*

He would have liked a child, a little girl perhaps, but Lili had insisted that she didn't want a baby. A child would have changed their lives too much; she didn't want the responsibility. Loving her dearly, he accepted her wishes. It helped that his parents were no longer alive, so they were not around to complain of the lack of grandchildren. Jinnan's and Lili's days were their own and they were long.

But as time went on, she began to find fault with him: the way he snored, the way he spat, the way he slept without washing his feet. He was hurt when she called him a 'peasant'.

However, no matter how hard things were, she loved to hear the words he sang so beautifully for the wedding ride. He had found her delight embarrassing; these were public words, part of a ceremony. He did care for her with all his heart, but these words had nothing to do with Lili and him.

But today he saw that he had been wrong; he now realized that all along he had indeed been singing about the two of them. All his feelings for her, all the hopes he once had for them, were expressed in these words of love and passion.

He put on a brave face, less for himself than for the carriers, who needed to be paid. 'The wind blows softly, the sun shines warmly,' he sang. 'With so much good fortune and so much joy, we wish you luck, and hope that you will grow your white hair together.'

'Hey! Hey!' the sedan carriers shouted together. The crowd gathered once again, to watch the final part of the event.

'Sedan down.' Jinnan's trembling voice rang out thinly. The right hand that had been holding the trumpet felt heavy and sore. This would be his last sedan job, he decided. He would rather go back to poorly paid and exhausting building work than suffer this pain.

The front of the sedan opened and the thin, southern-looking groom got out and stretched. Then he turned as if remembering something, just as the bride stepped out.

So it *was* her, Jinnan saw as their eyes met, although her eyes had tears in them, and her face seemed fixed and strangely unlined. He had heard about the operation that was available nowadays, to stretch the skin and make people look younger – Lili had even mentioned it. Now she did look younger, but old at the same time.

He thought she was going to fall, and stepped towards her. The southern man caught her and laughed. 'Well, that was fun. What shall we try next? I've heard the boat trip is good.'

She remained in his arms and murmured something. He nodded and reached into his pocket. 'How much do I owe you?' he asked Jinnan, slightly impatiently.

Jinnan stood there without moving; no words came out of his mouth. One of the carriers spoke for him. 'Five hundred and fifty yuan,' he said.

'Here, take six hundred.' The southern man pushed the money into Jinnan's hands and smiled. 'The extra's for your flowery words. You have a clever pair of lips.'

Jinnan's hands trembled and the money fell on the ground. One of the sedan men bent down and picked the notes up, hesitated and handed them back to Jinnan. The southern man wrapped his arm around Lili and led her away towards the bridge.

'Wait.' Suddenly Jinnan's voice rang out. 'You are supposed to put the money in a red wedding handkerchief.'

'What are you talking about?'

'It's the tradition.'

'Oh, come on, I gave you a tip.'

'That's not the point, you sat in a wedding sedan, so you pay me money wrapped in a red handkerchief.'

'You're being silly.'

'In a red handkerchief.'

'But we're not getting married!'

'You're . . . what?' Jinnan stared at Lili's pink wedding dress, and at all the traditional objects whose names sounded like 'early birth of a son', which he and his men had carefully placed in the sedan for the occasion.

'We rented the clothes at the Bright Light centre.' Lili's voice floated to him in a low whisper. 'My boyfriend just wanted to have some fun.'

The First Party

ATTIA HOSAIN

A story from India, retold by Clare West

*In India in the old days a young unmarried
woman would live in her parents' home, carefully
hidden away from the eyes of the world until the
time came for her to marry. If she went outside
the house, her clothes would hide her body from
the eyes of men and their desires. But times
change, customs change, people change . . .*

*A first party is usually an enjoyable, exciting
occasion, but not for this young wife . . .*

After the darkness of the verandah, the confusing brightness
of the room made the doorstep almost invisible, and she
nearly fell over it. Her nervousness was getting close to terror,
and she wished she could return to the friendly darkness, but
her husband was already pushing her gently into the room.

'My wife,' he said in English, and the sound of the foreign
words softened the awareness of this new relationship.

The tall, smiling woman came towards them with
outstretched hands, and the wife put her own weakly into
the other's firm hold.

'How d'you do?' said the woman.

'How d'you do?' said the fat man beside her.

'I am very well, thank you,' she said, in the low voice of an
uncertain child repeating a lesson. Her shy glance avoided their

eyes. They turned to her husband, and she stood there, in the warm current of their easy friendliness, coldly conscious of herself.

'I hope we are not too early,' her husband said.

'Of course not – the others are late. Do sit down.'

She sat on the edge of the big chair, her shoulders bent, nervously pulling her sari over her head.

'What will you drink?' the fat man asked her.

'Nothing, thank you.'

'Cigarette?'

'No, thank you.' She was sure that her husband and the tall woman were talking about her. She could feel needles of discomfort, and she smiled to hide them.

The tall woman held a wineglass in one hand and a cigarette in the other. She wondered how it felt to hold a cigarette with such self-confidence. The woman had long nails, pointed and bright red. She looked at her own – unpainted, cut carefully short – wondering how anyone could eat, work, wash with those claws tipped with blood. She drew her sari over her hands, covering her rings and bracelets, noticing the other's bare wrists, like a widow's.

'Shy little thing, isn't she, but charming,' said the woman, as if calming a frightened child.

'She'll get over it. Give me time,' her husband laughed. The wife heard him and blushed.

When other guests came in, she did not know whether she should stand up as they were being introduced. But her husband came and stood beside her, putting his hand on her shoulder, so she knew she must remain sitting.

She was glad when they forgot her for their drinks, their cigarettes, their talk and laughter. She drew back into her chair, lonely in her strangeness but hating the thought of anyone approaching her. She felt curious eyes on her, and this made her even more uncomfortable. When anyone came and sat by her, she smiled in cold defence, and her awkward answers soon cut short any conversation. She found people's talk difficult to follow, with their references to experiences she had not had. Even the women's conversation about dress and appearance seemed unfamiliar to her; she could not understand their interest in bodies, which she thought should be covered.

When she saw how simply they were dressed, she wished she had not put on her bright rich clothes and her heavy jewellery. She had done so because it was the custom to dress like that, but here no one seemed to care for customs, or even know them. Her discomfort changed to anger, and she stared at the strange creatures around her. But her quick eyes slipped shyly away if they met someone else's.

Her husband came, at intervals that grew longer, with a few cheerful words, or a friend to whom he proudly presented 'My wife'. She noticed the never-empty glass in his hand, and the smell of his breath, and from anxiety and shock she turned to disgust and anger. It was wicked to drink – their religion forbade it – and she could not forgive him.

She could not make herself smile any more, but no one noticed, and their unconcern made her angrier. She was tired of the continual 'Will you have a drink?', 'What will you drink?', 'Sure you won't drink?' It seemed they objected to her not drinking, while she objected to them drinking – she found this confusing. She asked for a glass of orange juice and used it as protection, putting it to her lips when anyone came near.

They were eating now, helping themselves from the table by the wall. She did not want to leave her chair, and wondered if it was wrong and they would notice she was not eating. A girl came towards her, offering her a plate of food. She sat up stiffly and took the plate with a smile.

'Do help yourself,' the girl said, bending forward. As her light sari slipped from her shoulder, each high breast was visible beneath her tight red silk blouse. The wife pulled her own sari closer round her, blushing. The girl, unaware, said, 'Try this sandwich, and the olives are good.'

She had never seen an olive before but did not want to admit it, and when she put it in her mouth, she wanted to spit it out. When no one was looking, she slipped it under her chair, then felt sure someone had seen her and would find it.

The room closed in on her with its noise and smoke. There was now the added loudness of music from the radiogram. She watched, fascinated, the movement of the machine as it changed records, but she hated the ugly sounds it threw at her. A girl walked up to it and started singing, moving her body along with the music. Her bare skin showed through the thin material she was wearing.

She felt angry again. These were disgusting, shameless, good-for-nothing girls, so free with men, their clothes drawing attention to their bodies instead of hiding them, with their painted false mouths and their short hair that looked like a mad woman's.

She fed her bitterness with every possible fault her mind could think of. These women were evil and wicked – they were trying to copy the foreigners, for whom she felt no hatred, because she expected nothing better from them. She wanted to break those records, the noise which they called music.

A few couples began to dance, when they had rolled aside the carpet. She felt a sick horror at the way the men held the women, at the closeness of their bodies, at their coarsely suggestive movements. That surely was the extreme limit of what was possible in the presence of others. Her mother had nearly died in childbirth and had not cried out in case the men outside might hear, and she, her child, had to see this show of . . . Her offended modesty stopped her completing the thought.

This was an attack on the basic rules which shaped her beliefs and which controlled her life. Protection against man's desire had always been necessary – not against touch alone, but also sound and sight.

A man came and asked her to dance, and she withdrew into her chair in horror, shaking her head. Her husband saw her and called out as he danced, 'Come on, don't be shy. You'll soon learn.'

She felt a flame of anger as she looked at him, and kept on shaking her head until the man left her, surprised by the violence of her refusal. She saw him dancing with another girl and knew they must be talking about her, because they looked towards her and smiled.

She was trembling with her complicated feelings of anger, hatred, jealousy, and confusion, when her husband walked up to her and pulled her lovingly by the hand.

'Get up. I'll teach you myself.'

She held tight to the chair as she struggled, and the violence of her reply, 'Leave me alone,' made him drop her hand with shocked surprise as the laughter left his face. She noticed his quick embarrassed glance round the room, then the hard anger of his eyes as he left her without a word. He laughed more loudly when he joined the others, to drown that moment's silence, but it wrapped its miserable emptiness around her.

She had been so sure of herself in her anger, dismissing these

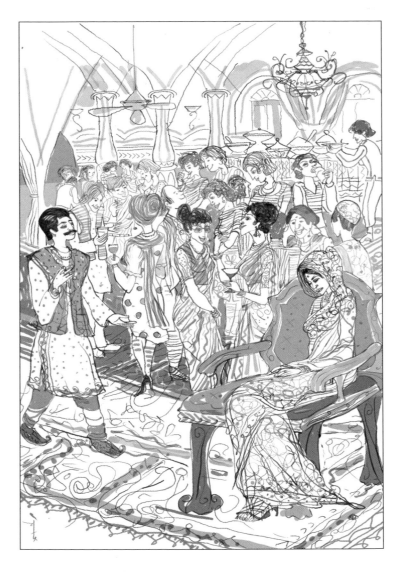

*She trembled with her complicated feelings of
anger, hatred, jealousy, and confusion.*

people as wrong. She was confident that her beliefs were right, because they were held by her parents and grandparents, and were centuries old. When she had seen them being attacked, in her mind they remained safe from destruction. Now she saw that her husband was one of the destroyers, and despite this, she knew that her life must for ever be part of his – it was the most important belief of all. In confusion and despair she was surrounded by ruins.

She wished desperately for the safety of the walled home from which her marriage had promised an adventurous escape. There, each strict rule became a guiding stone, marking a safe path through unknown dangers.

The tall woman came and sat beside her and put a hand kindly on her head.

'Tired, child?' The sympathy in her voice and eyes was unbearable.

She got up and ran to the verandah, put her head against a wooden post and wet it with her tears.

Fair Trade

PREETA SAMARASAN

A story from Malaysia, retold by Clare West

On a quiet, sleepy Malaysian island, the sun shines and the beaches are beautiful, but few tourists come. Life is hard. The islanders have little money and little hope for the future.

Then one day a yacht arrives, bringing tall, golden American models for a fashion shoot. Young Manju, who tells the story, soon realizes that life for her and her brother Murali will never be the same again . . .

When Mr and Mrs Hotel Kong first heard that the Straits Trading models were coming all the way from America to take photos on our island, they announced the news to everyone who was near enough the front desk to hear. 'Straits Trading,' they declared proudly. 'Even you haven't heard the name also, you've seen their clothes in magazines. All the famous people wear them.' And they ended their little speech by saying firmly, 'This is big news for our island. Big news.'

After the company sent their catalogues, Mrs Hotel Kong set them up like family photos on a table in reception. Such odd clothes the models wore in those pictures: worn out, mended dresses; blouses like rice sacks; shady hats for working in the fields. In the African photos their feet were bare, and in China they wore the rubber slip-on shoes we used to keep our feet safe from insects in our own backyards.

'So rich and dressing like beggars only,' my mother said in wonder.

None of us could quite believe it: a fashionable American company that could afford to travel all over the world, choosing the Paradise Hotel? It was not, after all, a luxury hotel, and it had hardly any of the traditional touches that appealed so much to tourists. But the barman did know how to make a Planter's Punch and a Singapore Sling, and the tourists still came for the Real Island Experience, ate the local specialities, and called the natural swimming pool charming (it was really just a rock-trapped bit of sea). If it weren't for the Paradise Hotel, our family would have been out of work, and as poor as the miserable people who lived on the other side of the island.

Our island had been in trouble for some time, and none of us really knew why. What we did know was that the flood of tourists had begun to dry up. The travellers who still came, the tired, unshaven ones who couldn't afford Phuket or Bali, were mean with their tips. They filled their stomachs with anything they could get for free. They pushed past us in and out of the local shops and bought nothing.

Half the town was out of work by the time my father lost his job. He'd been working for Mr Rajan at the spice factory for thirty years, so long that the spices he had breathed in were threatening to burst his body open from the inside. When he coughed you could smell the spices: chilli in the mornings; black pepper when he was angry; fenugreek when he was tired; cardamom on cool nights. Mr Rajan had a ready-made excuse for dismissing him: 'You cough more than you work, man,' he said. 'You going to spread your illness over the whole island. One of our spice bags is seventy-five percent your insides and only twenty-five percent our spices.'

After my father was sacked, he sat and coughed in his armchair all day. If you listened quietly outside the sitting room, you could hear him mutter to himself between coughs: 'Useless, useless. What is all this for?' The coughing made the sweat pour from his skin, so that all his shirts turned yellow under the arms. His hair permanently stood up in the places where it pressed against the chair when he fell asleep.

All across our island, other men lay in other armchairs, although they were not coughing. They stared miserably at their waterstained ceilings. But we had more money than most; my mother and my brother Murali managed to earn a tiny amount at the hotel, even when things were at their worst. My mother cleaned the tourists' red hairs out of their shower and changed their meaty-smelling sheets; my brother served them drinks in the bar-restaurant after school.

Then the Straits Trading company contacted Mr Hotel Kong. Straightaway he hired workmen to paint and repair the hotel. 'Now we put in small money,' he said, 'tomorrow we get big money. Where they gonna eat and drink if not here, in our restaurant and our bar? I tell you, after this island is famous, different kind of tourist gonna come here. Good for everybody, not just me. They will spend their money on our island, yes or not? Straits Trading is no chicken-feed company! I promise you one thing,' he added grandly, looking around at the crowd gathered round him, 'in one week these people will completely change our life.'

'Boss is living in a dream world,' my mother muttered to Hamid the cook. But in her voice I could hear a touch of impossible hope: maybe, just maybe Mr Hotel Kong really did know how the world worked, and we were all on the edge of something unimaginably wonderful.

Only my father refused to believe. 'If it's so easy for the westerners to change our lives,' he said furiously, 'why is half the world still starving? Why are there babies dying in Africa and India? Don't think just because they got white skin they're gods. They're selfish and useless, just like the rest of us.'

The Straits Trading models came in a blue-and-white sailing boat that cut silently through the still afternoon water, and when we saw them in the distance we all rushed onto the beach to watch: Mr and Mrs Hotel Kong, me and Murali and our mother, Hamid the cook, Jeevan the pool boy, the barman, the cleaners and gardeners, Mrs Hotel Kong's two dogs – and all of us were suddenly speechless. Of course we had all seen white people before. But at the Paradise Hotel there had never been anyone like the golden creatures who appeared from their boat on that bright December day. The women got out, legs first like in an old American film, legs so fine and delicate it took them thirty seconds to unfold themselves, like brand-new insect wings. Mr Hotel Kong did not breathe as he offered his arm to each of them. Jeevan the pool boy moved slowly forward, as if unconscious.

'Foof!' Murali said. He had pictures of women like these under his bed at home.

They were long and thin as water insects, but they had a slow, snake-like way of walking. They had shiny hair and sharp cheekbones. Their skin was like oil, so smooth it caught the light when they moved. There were six women and two men and you could tell the men liked it that way. The men wore open-chested shirts, tight white trousers and sunglasses, and they laughed a lot, at things the women said or at nothing at all. And all of them, the men and the women, had a lot of white teeth. Straight teeth, all the same size, not like ours and not like the teeth of the white people we'd seen.

'Look at that one,' my brother said, pointing at a girl in stripey, see-through trousers. 'Wearing pyjamas in the daytime until can see her panties also!' It was true, the girl's long legs showed through her trousers, but all the same, panties was not a nice word to say in front of people. I looked at the girl to see if she'd heard us. She hadn't; she was talking to another girl, leaning towards her and smiling.

You could feel our sudden certainty in the air, a stillness followed by a quickening, a drawing in of breath: at once all of us standing there were sure that all the castles we'd built in the air were achievable after all. Our dreams really were going to come true: look at these shiny people, arriving like a grand film opening with curvy letters and big music. Look at them.

That night we could talk of nothing else. 'Soooo tall those girls are,' my mother said in wonder at the dinner table, 'Mr Hotel Kong comes up to below their shoulders only!' She put a ball of rice-and-fish firmly into her mouth and took the bones from between her teeth.

'Supermodels, what,' Murali said. 'Don't you know, in America, everything is super? Market is not good enough for them so they got supermarket. Superman, Superstar, Superbowl. Supermodels. Cindy Crawford Claudia Skiffer Heidi Nice-bum Klum Linda Angel Evangel—'

'What is all this nonsense?' growled my father, and before any of us could answer, his left hand flew across the table and smacked Murali on the side of the head. Then he lowered his eyes and spoke without looking at any of us, the words pouring out onto his plate to mix thickly with his uneaten rice-and-fish. 'Instead of reading your rubbish magazines,' he growled, 'how about seeing if you can do some odd jobs for those westerners? Wasn't Kong boasting nicely about how many jobs would be opening up? You know what is happening to us and still you sit around and dream about women with no clothes on!'

Murali opened his mouth; then he closed it, and his mouth tightened. 'Be nice to your Appa,' our mother had told us only recently. 'Be patient and don't talk back. He's the only Appa you've got.' Of course, we'd been told not to talk back before, and we'd seldom listened. We were complainers and deniers, always asking why and how. But this time we'd heard her voice in our ears, and we'd both looked up to see her looking sadly at her cleaning-lady hands. The delicate perfume of cardamom was hanging in the evening air; we'd been able to hear our father coughing, coughing, coughing in the sitting room.

Now our mother said after a while, 'Maybe your Appa is right. No harm in asking those people if they have any extra jobs. After all you have some free time in the afternoons.' She looked at Murali, then at me, and finally at our father. 'Who knows?' she said. 'Maybe Mr and Mrs Hotel Kong were right, isn't it? After all, those people have money to spend.'

Our father's burst of anger saddened no one more than himself. That night he refused to go to bed. He sat in the living room with his hands over his eyes, and although the lights were all out, his face shone in the moonlight. All night long he coughed in his armchair, once so violently that the chair moved. He muttered and sighed like an old man struggling to do something that had once been easy. In the morning, he was at the table when we came out into the kitchen. He was unwashed and uncombed as usual, but in his open right hand he held his cat's eye ring. He cleared his throat.

'Murali,' he said simply, 'you keep this ring from now on.'

Murali frowned and said, 'Hanh? What for I want that ring?'

My father had had that cat's eye ring since he was eighteen. It was the one object of any worth that our family owned, but we could never sell it. Although we were not rich, we had our pride and our past, all contained in that one ring. My father's mother had kept the ring for him after his father died, and on his eighteenth birthday she'd given it to him. Our grandfather had inherited the ring from his father, and our great-grandfather from his father before that, and it was whispered – although our mother always said, 'Tsk, all that simply-simply people say' – that our great-great-grandfather had killed someone to get that jewel.

The cat's eye was so large and so silky that if it hadn't been stolen, my father had always claimed, it would surely have ended up in the engagement ring of some English queen. Among our people, cat's eyes were said to protect the wearer from evil spirits. My father's stone was of the very finest quality, a rich yellowy color on one side, and milky on the other. It was set so deep into the ring that its milky bottom touched the skin of the wearer, because a jewel that did not touch its wearer would not protect him fully.

'Just keep it,' our father said now. 'It is good for our family. The man of the family should have it.'

It's true that I could never have had that ring anyway. It was the men's duty to guard it, just as the women and girls were all precious jewels to protect from strangers' desiring eyes. In the pale morning light of our kitchen the cat's eye looked narrowly at me, as if we two shared a secret. I stood there, breathless, behind Murali, but I did not want him to take it. If he did, if it passed from my father's hand to his, that would mean everything had changed. My father's black hair would turn white before my eyes. His back would bend; his bones would stiffen. He would sit in his armchair and wait to die.

I'm not the man of the family yet, I wanted Murali to say. You keep it, Appa.

Instead he only said, 'Tsk, all this what for?' His voice was rough, and he took the ring quickly from my father's hand, but he rubbed the stone with both his thumbs before putting it on. Then he sat down to eat his bread and butter.

The ring brought my brother luck he could never have imagined. When he went to ask Mrs Hotel Kong if the Straits Trading people might need an odd-job boy, she offered him something even better. 'Stand straight,' she said. 'Let me see how tall are you.' She looked at him very critically from head to toe and back again before she said, 'You should be okay. They're looking for a few local boys to take photos of, with the models. For sure they'll pay you nicely. I asked the pool boy also, and two-three waiters. No need to do anything also, simply sit and smile and they'll pay you, man! Easy money.'

So my brother went to talk to the photographers, and they too looked up and down his thin brown body and said, 'Okay, fine, come back tomorrow at four o'clock.' It was that easy. My brother was going to be a model – not super, maybe, but a real model, in photos with white-and-gold girls on a beach.

They didn't need girl models, but no one said anything the next day when I sat watching them. A lady came to give Murali and Jeevan fresh clothes to wear: a black shirt for Murali, a white shirt for Jeevan. Exactly the same shorts for both.

And then, at four thirty, the pyjama girl with the long legs appeared at the top of the outdoor staircase. She wasn't wearing see-through pyjamas now, though. Her hair was brushed up so that it made an even bigger, brighter cloud than usual. Her blouse was made of tiny pieces of fine, torn cloth sewn together, and her trousers were like a soldier's, grass-green and full of pockets. Strangest of all was this: with that funny torn-up blouse and those soldier's trousers, she wore the most delicate high-heels I'd ever seen. They were so high that inside those shoes the girl stood on her toes as though there was almost nothing keeping her tied to the ground, and she might take off any minute now and fly away above our heads, forcing Murali and Jeevan to turn their necks to try and get a look at what lay under her blouse.

She descended, her heels sounding on each metal stair, and when she got to the bottom we all realized that it was her we'd been waiting for, without knowing it. The air smelled like no perfume I'd ever smelled: not an eye-watering smell like Mrs Hotel Kong's perfume, or a heavy pink smell like the rosewater my mother wore for weddings. It was faint and slightly sad, like flowers just around the corner, but each time you turned the corner expecting to see them, they'd be around the next corner after all.

The girl ran both her hands through her hair, smiled first at Jeevan and then at my brother, and said, 'Hi guys, I'm Alice.'

Hi guys, I'm Alice. It was only four words, but I knew what they really meant. When Mr Hotel Kong had told us that the Straits Trading people would change our lives, he must have meant Alice. Although he hadn't yet seen her at the time, he must have thought of a girl just like Alice, with her yellow eyes full of promise, her skin like a new day, her special smell. I breathed deep. My nose tried to grab that smell from the air and hold it in my throat. All the possibility of those four words, everything that Alice had seen and touched and carried in her blood rushed through my head: fast cars, white wedding cakes, horses, cream-colored carpets, lifts full of buttons, trumpets, violins, snow. Anything was possible.

My brother and Jeevan only smiled shyly back at Alice then, but for days afterwards they greeted each other with a sexy 'Hi guys', Jeevan making a snake-like movement, my brother running his hands through his hair. Then they would walk slowly up and down the poolside, and each time they passed each other they'd say 'Hi guys' again, and lick their lips temptingly, or touch a finger to their chins. 'I'm Alice,' one of them would finally say, the fourth or fifth time they passed each other, and then the other would repeat it – 'I'm Alice' – and then they would bend over and hit each other's backs and laugh wildly until they fell flat on the ground.

On that afternoon, though, when Alice said 'Hi guys,' Jeevan just smiled at Murali, Murali smiled back at Jeevan, and then they both smiled their uneven-toothed smiles at Alice.

I could tell you that Alice was even more beautiful close-up than she was from far away in her pyjamas, but beautiful is just a word for things that belong where they are. Beautiful is for Hamid the cook's daughter doing her evening candle dances for the tourists. Beautiful is for the silk saris that used to arrive at our island shops. The long white beach at sunset, dark trees and fire-red water, that's beautiful too. Alice was from another world. She smelled different. She talked different. All the colors of her – her reddish hair, her purple lips, her yellow eyes – stood out against the greens and browns of our island. In a way, Alice looked all wrong sitting there for the photographer on the steps of the Paradise Hotel between my brother and Jeevan the pool boy, but it was a delicious wrongness. It made my fingertips hurt and my mouth dry, and I could tell from the way Jeevan's and my brother's toes curled on the bare ground that it did something very similar to them.

The photographer made Alice sit on the steps that led up to the hotel, with Jeevan and my brother on either side of her. Yet it was as if Alice wasn't there at all, as if she were just in my imagination, because my brother and Jeevan could only look at each other, like two young male lions ready for a good fight, eager and jumpy, the one just slightly smaller than the other. Between them Alice leaned back on her hands and narrowed her eyes lazily, as if the very air she breathed was different, as if it were cooler, thinner, cleaner, like the air on a mountain top.

Our story was becoming a proper story, and it began like this:

Once upon a time we lived on a foot-shaped island forgotten even by the tourists, until one day a golden girl named Alice discovered us and changed everything.

I didn't know exactly how this story would end, but of course there would be a 'happily ever after', with sandwiches and bottled drinks and music. At the very least, business at the hotel would improve. I saw my father get out of bed and stand up straight and stop coughing because times were better and there was nothing to cough about any more. I saw my brother going to the cinema theatre with Alice. Then I saw Alice sending us letters and parcels from America. Maybe even tickets to visit her in New York. Who could say?

'Such a pretty girl,' Mrs Hotel Kong said every few minutes when she came out to see how the photographers were getting on, and all of us wished she'd shut up, because it was both unnecessary and a bad thing to say, like gossiping about God.

'Well?' our father said in between coughs that night. 'All okay? They paid you already?'

My brother drew his breath in and leaned forward. I could tell he wanted to put it all into words my father would understand. He wanted to grab our father by the collar of his sweat-stained shirt and pull him into that other world he'd discovered, in which the beach would never again be the same because Alice had stood on its sand; in which Alice's eyes were a whole different color in the sun; in which clothes were just for taking pictures in, and people said things like 'Hi guys.'

Instead he only lowered himself back down onto his heels and muttered, 'Not yet. They said they'll pay at the end. Still got plenty of work for me.'

There was a second day of pictures: pictures of Alice and three other girls in the flame-of-the-forest tree by the swimming pool while Jeevan removed leaves from its surface; pictures of Alice feeding the fish while my brother watched her from the other side of the pool; pictures of Alice leaning out of an upstairs window while Jeevan the pool boy pretended to play a guitar he'd had to be taught how to hold and my brother watched from across the yard, far away, outside the picture, unnoticed this time by the photographer. In the shadow of the tree my brother looked lonely and chicken-chested, like a small boy last in the shop queue for ice cream.

'I know something,' I said to Murali at the end of the third day. I kicked the backs of his ankles as we walked home.

'Ah, shaddup your mouth,' he shot back, perhaps because he knew what I was going to say.

'You like Alice,' I said. 'Like that.'

He wheeled around and pushed me lightly away. 'No need to talk like you know everything, okay? Twelve years old and already acting like a woman. Go away and leave me alone for five minutes, can't you?'

'You going to ask her to marry you? You going to go back to America with her?'

In those days, you see, I loved to annoy Murali like that. He almost expected it. 'My little sister. I had to bring her,' he would say to his friends. These were our ways not only of

My brother had discovered another world, in which clothes were just for taking pictures in, and people said things like 'Hi guys.'

entertaining ourselves but of keeping order in our world. So I
didn't expect what followed: Murali grabbing me by my collar,
shaking me like he – almost like he wanted to shake the life out
of me.

'You didn't hear me, is it?' he said. 'You didn't understand or
what? Didn't I ask you to go away and leave me alone?'

'Yah,' I said, 'yah I understand,' but Murali was shaking me
so hard I couldn't hear my own words. It wasn't the shaking
that most confused me, though; it was the tiny tears I saw in
the corners of Murali's eyes when I looked fearfully up into
them. I'd never seen Murali cry: by the time I was old enough
to notice, he was past the age of crying.

When Alice came to find us by the swimming pool on the third
day, I knew it wasn't just us who wanted to be in her presence;
she wanted to be our friend too. We'd been helping Jeevan
the pool boy remove the dead leaves from the swimming-pool
surface. 'Hi guys,' one of them would say every so often. 'I'm
Alice,' the other would respond, sticking his chest out.

'Hey!' Alice said when she saw Jeevan and Murali, but she
was laughing.

My brother stood suddenly straight and shot her a nervous
smile. But Jeevan was clever and confident, and he knew how
to pull anyone into a joke. 'Hi guys,' he said, half-turning his
body sexily towards Alice, 'I'm Jeevan.' Then Alice hit him on
the shoulder and burst out laughing, and my brother slowly
joined in, and before long they were jumping around in the
sunshine, throwing leaves at each other, shouting and laughing
and copying each other. And whether it was because Alice had
touched him first, or because his joke had been so successful,
Jeevan suddenly dared to touch her. He pulled her hair like a

naughty schoolboy; he pulled her nose; and then – it made me catch my breath, and I could almost hear my brother catching his – he picked her up and threatened to throw her into the swimming pool.

Of course we all knew he wouldn't. Even Alice knew he wouldn't, because she was too clean and lovely to spoil, but she kicked all the same, and screamed until he put her down at the very last moment, just as Mrs Hotel Kong's heels came noisily out onto the poolside.

'My goodness!' she said, 'What you all doing here? Make me trip and fall in these shoes, then you know! That worried I was. What you doing here? Hanh?'

'Oh, nothing,' Alice said breathlessly.

'Nothing, Madam,' said Jeevan. He'd somehow managed to continue removing the leaves from the pool after putting Alice down, so that it looked now as though he'd been interrupted in the middle of a working afternoon like any other.

After Mrs Hotel Kong left, Alice and Jeevan turned to look at each other again, and they stared at each other for so long they might have been having a staring competition. And when they started laughing they started at exactly the same moment, so that neither one of them could claim to have won. But it was Murali who looked like the real loser, standing there scratching his head, trying not to look at Jeevan and Alice, our father's ring too big and heavy for his hand.

I stood up. I was about to go and pull at my brother's sleeve and tell him that it was time we went to find our mother and go home, when just like that, like a bored little girl, Alice turned away from Jeevan, and, putting her face up close to my brother's and her hand on his cheek, said, 'You're a good boy, aren't you? You're not a bad boy like that one!' My brother smiled a smile I'd never seen before, and I knew he was only just discovering what I'd seen two days before: he was real now, a real boy with a proper story. Things were happening to him.

And so both of us wondered: what if, after all the world's wonders had always been out of our reach, we really could have Alice? Our hard lives, the hot sun and shapeless days, even the occasional hunger would be bearable – if we had Alice.

'If I tell your father,' our mother said after she found Murali in Alice's room the following day, 'now he'll drop dead.'

'We didn't do anything,' Murali protested, 'just watching TV only.'

'Just watching TV! Sitting there in the bed like a newly married couple. I know that type of girl. Nicely-nicely she has wrapped you around her little finger and you've fallen for her nonsense. What you think, these white girls—'

'Alice isn't that type of girl.'

'Oho, how sweetly her name comes in your mouth now, Alish Alish Alish, Alish this Alish that, as if you've been best friends all your life. How you know what type of girl she is, anyway? Hanh? You are not the one spending eight hours in the hotel every day, seeing with your own eyes what goes on behind people's doors. In the mornings the swimming pool boy is sleeping with his head on her knees and in the afternoons she is sitting with her head on your shoulder. Now you tell me, what type of girl is she?'

Murali had no answer to that, and neither he nor my mother said anything the rest of the way home. That night he turned restlessly over and over in his bed, and once I even heard him cry into his pillow. And the next day neither Alice nor Jeevan the pool boy was anywhere to be seen, though Murali and I looked for them everywhere.

This is what I sacrificed for my brother's sake: ten minutes of my time and a small amount of pride. And what I risked: a smack from my mother if she found out.

I would like to tell you that I did what I did because I felt I owed it to my brother for having made him cry. That I was unselfish enough to think: for once let one of us have some happiness, and never mind if it isn't me. But the truth is that I wanted Alice for myself just as much as for Murali. I wanted to be able to make bigger and bigger boasts before the other girls at school: Alice and my brother went to see a film together. Alice and my brother went to the Paris Je Taim Cafe for ice creams. Alice is my brother's girlfriend. I practised saying this last in front of the mirror, watching the f of girlfriend steam up the glass.

'Alice!' I whispered when I managed to catch her alone. I'd waited outside her door while my brother helped out at the bar, and now, finally, here she was, wrapped in a bath towel, her curls pulled long and loose by her swim.

'Hello, baby,' she said, as if she'd been expecting to find me there.

Alice, Alice, I longed to say, my name is Manju. But I had no time to waste; Alice was a busy girl. Already I heard rubber shoes coming up the outdoor staircase, probably one of her friends coming to remind her of their strict timetable. 'Alice,' I said, 'you know or not, my brother likes you?'

In Tamil films, this is when the heroine would have given a modest little laugh and lowered her eyes, perhaps even hidden her face with a corner of her bath towel. Alice did none of these things; she reached out and pulled my hair and said, 'And I like you! What do you say to that?'

What did I say to that? I was still making my brain work

overtime, thinking of some way to grab this conversation and force it back onto the correct path, when Alice's friend appeared, breathing fast, in the corridor.

'Hey Alice—' she began.

'Look, Kate, it's that guy Mu-rah-li's little sister,' said Alice. 'Isn't she so pretty?'

The two of them stood there looking at me, laughing in the wrong way, sending each other meaningful glances of whose meaning I alone was unsure.

'We gotta go,' Kate said at last. 'We're already ten minutes late.'

'All right,' said Alice. 'Gimme FIVE minutes. Bye, little sister!' Grabbing Kate by the elbow, she disappeared into her room and left me looking at her locked door. And that was that, the end of my attempt to arrange – what? I hadn't even been sure. I'd thought Alice would blush, and our conversation would result in a plan. A secret meeting, a promise to deliver her letters to Murali without my parents' knowledge after she went back to America. But I had no Plan B.

A week after we'd gathered on the beach to watch the Straits Trading Company arrive, we gathered again to see them depart. There they all were: the men in tight white trousers and the models. As Alice passed Jeevan she gave him a little push, and he pushed her back. She was wearing a bright yellow dress which opened all the way up to her bum, and when she stepped into the boat with Mr Hotel Kong's help I saw a flash of her red panties. I looked at Murali out of the corner of my eye, but he said nothing, though he was staring so hard at Alice I knew he must have seen them too. Alice was leaning towards the girl beside her to say something just as the photographer shut the door behind her. Then both girls looked at Murali and laughed until they had to cover their faces. Murali smiled at them, but they weren't looking. As the engine started up Alice turned and waved. Her eyes, suddenly serious, were on the blue-and-yellow sign above our heads that said Paradise Hotel. She bit her lower lip and stared fixedly at that sign.

When the yacht was a small white splash in the distance, I pulled at Murali's hand to wake him from his daydream. He tried to take it away from me, but I refused to let it go. My fingers tightened around his, and when I lifted his hand to my face to look at it, I saw that my father's ring was gone.

'Murali!' I whispered. 'What happened to Appa's ring?'

'Fell into the drain,' he said, turning away.

The idea of it – my father's ring, carried away with plastic bags and kitchen rubbish on the brown water of an underground drain – sat at the top of my throat, cold as a block of ice that would hurt my stomach if I tried to swallow it. But then, suddenly, I knew what he'd done. 'You gave it to Alice!' I whispered in horror. I remember stepping away from him then, but I was not too frightened to go on, 'Yes or not? Tell the truth!' Yes, he'd given the ring to Alice because his tongue wasn't as quick as Jeevan's. All he'd had was that ring, and he'd hoped it would be enough.

Around us the little crowd was breaking up, Mrs Hotel Kong returning to her front desk, my mother hurrying upstairs to pull the sheets off the models' empty beds, Jeevan lying down for a sleep by the pool. Still Murali wouldn't look at me. 'Manju,' he said finally – so seldom did he say my name that his mouth made a funny shape around the word, and he himself paused and frowned – 'why can't you mind your own business?'

I would tell our mother, I decided. She would tell Mrs Hotel

Kong, who would get the ring back from Alice. Alice was Alice, after all, and a thousand rings more beautiful than my father's lay in her future, with handsome men to give them to her. Our ring had been in our family for more than a hundred years, and our good luck depended on it. If my father found out it was gone he would lay his head in his hands and cough himself sadly to death. Far away in New York, Alice would know nothing of it.

But the ring, furious at being given away like a cheap toy, had already begun to destroy what remained of our fortune. When I went home to wait for my mother, I found my father rolling desperately around like a fish on the floor, as cardamom-perfumed liquid worked its way up from his lungs and out through his mouth. I ran back to the Paradise Hotel, and Mrs Hotel Kong called an ambulance. My mother sat beside my father in the back of the ambulance as it drove away. 'Go and find your brother,' she said, 'and you two come to the hospital in a taxi.'

Murali was still on the beach where I'd left him. Up and down he walked against the setting sun, his hands joined behind his back like an old man's. I stood watching him, breathing that cool, salty air, trying to work up into my mouth a single sentence that would say everything. I wanted him to know that we had no time for quarrels. That I needed him now. That I therefore forgave him. But I could hardly bear to look at that thin dark figure on the sand. My eyes kept turning to the quiet, shining water behind him, and all I could think about was my father's ring, sailing further and further out to sea on a white girl's hand.

Mid-Autumn

HWEE HWEE TAN

A story from Singapore, retold by Clare West

Parents often make sacrifices for their children. Perhaps they work long hours at difficult jobs in order to pay for expensive toys, fashionable clothes, a good education. And they hope, of course, for grateful, dutiful children.

In Singapore it is the Mid-Autumn Festival. A mother has made a traditional mooncake for her daughter, but her daughter has now grown up and is far away, in another continent, living under a different moon . . .

I wonder if she remembers the Mid-Autumn Festival? It is the fifteenth day of the eighth month, when the moon shines the brightest. I eat the mooncake I baked for my daughter.

I hoped she would appear on the doorstep – surprise! But no. Instead she smiled out from the photo she sent, spreading her bloodied hands beside the brick kiln in another continent.

The mooncake, if don't eat, must throw away. But like that waste money, very *gek sim*. Whenever I lose money, it makes me *gek sim* – it hurts my heart. So I eat the mooncake for her.

Most Singaporeans are happy during the Mid-Autumn Festival. The children's red paper lanterns swing from wooden sticks, and the candles inside the lanterns throw out little flashes of red light. But the festival makes me *gek sim*.

Fourteen years ago I bought my daughter a lantern. It was not like mine. I make my lanterns. Candle lanterns weren't good enough for my daughter. She ran around outside our house, holding one – then the wind blew out her candle. 'Candle so inconvenient,' she said. 'Mummy, Mummy, buy me that plastic Mickey Mouse lantern. It got battery. Wind no problem.'

'Ai-ya, when the Chinese beat the Mongolian government, where they got battery Mickey Mouse lanterns?' I said. I shook my head. You send a child to an English school in Singapore, they only want Mickey Mouse and McDonalds.

I reminded my daughter what the lantern meant. In the mid-seventeenth century, the Manchu army attacked our city, Yangzhou, killing many of the people and taking away all their weapons. Our Chinese ancestors planned to fight back, and secretly they made their own weapons. The only problem was, how to get the villagers to attack the enemy at the same time? During the Mid-Autumn Festival, they hid messages in the mooncakes passed on from neighbour to neighbour. 'When you see the lantern,' the message said, 'rise and fight!' That night, all over China, matches were lit, filling the villages with the light of red lanterns.

'The lantern reminds you,' I told my daughter, 'to grab back your weapons, fight for your freedom.'

My husband said, 'Don't be so mean.' He always accuses me of that. 'Buy her the lantern. She got one hundred for her science exam, reward her a bit.'

We bought the lantern. She ran to the playground with her Mickey Mouse lantern. I waited at Ah Kow's coffee-shop.

'Give me the usual,' I told Ah Kow.

Ah Kow poured the coffee from one cup into another, four times, to cool the coffee.

An English lesson played on television:

'*Ta yau chou.*' (Beep) 'She wants to go.'

'*Ta chou.*' (Beep) 'She goes.'

'*Ta chou le.*' (Beep) 'She has gone.'

My daughter returned. 'I'm thirsty.'

I ordered Ovaltine. Ah Kow didn't cool the Ovaltine because he only did that trick for coffee. I poured the steaming Ovaltine into the saucer. I blew lightly on it, and put my tongue in the saucer. 'Cool enough,' I said.

She lifted the saucer to her lips.

'Where's your Mickey Mouse?' I asked.

'Playground.'

'Stupid! Tell you to always keep it with you but you never listen.' I ran to the playground and looked everywhere. I dug into the sand in search of the lantern.

'Someone stole your lantern! Your new lantern!'

'Mummy, don't be sad, can always buy new one.'

'Ai-ya, so *gek sim*.' I put my hand against my heart. 'New lantern – just bought today. So *gek sim*.'

'Do you know what this means?' I said. It was a few months after my daughter lost her lantern, and a few months before she took her primary school leaving exams. She was eleven.

I pointed to the letter. 'When you see this picture on a letter, it means if the government tells you to do something, you cannot say no. Never mind if you taught secondary school science for ten years. Government just change the rules, say you must move down to teach primary school because you didn't study at university.' I folded the letter. 'I could have gone to university – I could have been a doctor. But no money, so no go. Go teach primary school instead.'

I put my hand on my daughter's pile of homework books and exam papers. 'Mummy will pay for your education. You study hard, you can go to any university. Then you won't get this type of letter.'

I used to be a very good secondary school teacher. But now I can't do the job I love. Instead, I teach those monkeys at Yat Sen Primary. Even if I put the right words on the board, they get the answers wrong. These children can't even copy. Take Haslinda, for example. She still can't read – how to teach children like that? I told her parents to send her to a special school, but her father's job is buying old newspapers and reselling them to the paper factories. 'Where I got money to send Haslinda to a special school?' he asked me.

I stayed in my teaching job so I could afford the best education for my daughter. I sent her to Methodist Girls' School, one of the best schools in Singapore. I paid for her art, piano, dancing, and Chinese classes. My husband says, 'When I was young, I never needed Chinese classes, never went to dancing.' So I paid for my daughter's classes myself.

Once, I wanted to run away. My daughter was ten. We had moved into the new flat in Bedok that *I* bought – my husband didn't pay a cent. When I came home after teaching, I had to mark homework books, ring the parents of children who had missed school, cook, clean the floor, and wash the clothes.

I hung the washing on the pole. I put the pole in the holder outside the window. In the flat above, my neighbours had their washing poles out. The water from their clothes fell onto mine, and made them even wetter.

My husband told me what he had done with our new flat.

I decided to run away, get a new job and a new life. As I left the building, I passed under the washing poles. Drops of water fell from the wet clothes on to the ground. My daughter was at the window. She screamed. The drops hit my neck. They were her tears. I looked at the round brown water marks on the ground. I shook my head – no, it was water from the wet clothes. But it felt like her tears rained on me.

I returned.

The day my daughter finished medical school, I thought – now she can be a doctor, make big money, find a good husband.

We went to Ah Kow's coffee-shop to celebrate. We sat down on the shaky chairs at our usual table. Ah Kow so mean. He makes big money ever since he went from selling coffee to food – he has a Rolex and a Mercedes – but he still uses the old chairs from ten years ago.

Ah Kow pushed the dirty plastic plates and glasses noisily together, and lifted them up with his right arm. His left hand, holding a dirty grey tablecloth, slid around the wooden table, wiping the coffee stains, and brushing fish and chicken bones onto the pile of dirty dishes.

'What you want?' he said.

I gave him my order – the best, most expensive dishes I knew. 'My daughter got her degree today,' I told him. 'She's going to be a doctor.'

'So smart,' Ah Kow clapped my daughter's back. 'When I sick, I come see you, you give me good price? I go cook for you now.' He walked to the kitchen.

My daughter bit her thumb. 'I'm not going to be a doctor. I'm going to be a missionary. In Uganda.'

I stared at her.

'When I was at Methodist Girls' School,' she said, 'a Ugandan church worker came to talk to us. She said she was dying of a terrible disease. Her husband had died, and the week before, she heard that her niece—'

My husband stood up. 'I work all through the night, drive taxi until I get night blindness, so you can study to be a doctor. You so ungrateful, don't want to stay in Singapore and take care of me, want to go take care of black people.'

'How can I be like the other doctors here, with their mobile phones, golf weekends, and social clubs, while people are dying in Uganda?'

'You go to Uganda,' my husband said, 'and this will be the last meal you have with us.'

Ah Kow was cooking in his tiny kitchen at one end of the coffee-shop. Clouds of steam poured from his pots and pans and filled the room.

'The smoke is getting to me,' my daughter said.

I followed her outside. It was the Mid-Autumn Festival. Tiny red lights flashed in the dark.

I shook my head. 'Ai-ya, so *gek sim*, so unhappy.'

'He can't stop me.'

'No, I mean your lantern make me *gek sim*.'

'What lantern?'

'Your Mickey Mouse lantern. See those red lights? That's the children at the playground, where you lost your lantern.'

My daughter took my hand. 'I know you're upset—'

'Your new lantern,' I said. 'So expensive – five dollars. You lost it the same day we bought it. So *gek sim*.' I put my hand to my heart.

'Forget the lantern. I'll write to you every week – no, twice a week. I'll tell you everything.'

'That's your problem. We buy everything for you. Whenever you lose something, you say, "Forget it, can always buy new one." You go to Uganda – what if they have war there? Soldiers blow up your house, you cannot come to Mummy and ask me to buy you a new house.'

'I'm not a child, I can take care of myself.'

'I know you can take care of yourself. Your problem is that you don't value what you have. You have something valuable, but when you lose it, you say, "Forget it, never mind." When I lose something, it make me *gek sim*, for always.'

'Where you going to get money to work in Uganda?' I said.

My daughter tells me – God's eye is even on a tiny bird, so He will provide for her.

I say, 'Ai-ya, looking after birds not difficult. You know what birds eat? Insects. You going to live on Ugandan insects?'

My daughter thinks she can bear being poor. What does she know about it, when I always give her nice food? When I won a book prize at school, my father brought me to Ah Kow's coffee-shop and ordered a slice of bread and butter. Butter was special for us in those days. That Prize Day morning, Ah Kow brought out butter fresh from the freezer. My father cut a thick slice, clapped it on white bread, and put sugar on top. He poured my Ovaltine into the saucer, and cooled it with his breath. I heard the noise my teeth made on the frozen butter and sugar. I washed it down with Ovaltine. That was my biggest treat.

My daughter eats butter whenever she likes. She has fresh milk. In my time, Nestlé powdered milk was unaffordable.

My daughter tells me she can bear being poor. 'The Church will pay my salary. And people give money to missionaries.'

'But like that, where got financial independence?'

She does not say anything. She does not seem worried.

I told her something I never told anyone before. It was the only way to stop her from making my mistakes. Before this day, when I told her anything important, I would wear a jacket, a white blouse and a dark grey skirt – teacher clothes. She would sit and I would stand in front of her.

Now I lay on my bed in pyjamas. My daughter stood in front of me, arms folded.

'That night I fought with your father – you were ten. He took twenty thousand dollars from my bank account.'

'How can he just take your money?'

'I have a joint account with your father – we can both use the money in it.'

My daughter frowned.

I lowered my head. 'I remember one time a colleague said, "My money is my money. What woman is stupid enough to open a joint account with her husband?" Well, I am that woman.'

My daughter shook her head.

I pulled the blanket over my chest. 'I paid for our flat in Bedok. Two months later, your father sold the flat, took the money and put it in his own account. He made me buy a new flat in Clementi. If I'd kept the money from the flat in Bedok, I could retire now. No more teaching those monkeys.'

'Tomorrow we'll open a separate bank account for you.'

I shook my head. 'When you have no financial independence, you have no weapon, no protection. You get trapped with a bad husband, a bad job. I slave away so you can study to be a doctor, make big money. Now you're going to throw it all away. You want to be poor, dependent, trapped.'

My daughter doesn't understand my husband. He had to give his money to his father. He kept his money only after he married me. Now it's his turn to take all his wife's and child's money. If my daughter goes to Uganda, he can't take her money. He thinks this is unjust. But I am in Singapore and he will never let go of my money.

What else could I say to stop her from leaving me? When my parents told me to do something, I obeyed. They said, 'Go university for what? Waste of money. Get a job.' I became a teacher. I know my daughter is not like me – she has her degree, she's not married. But what else could I say?

I held on to the chair beside me. 'I forbid you.'

'I need to do this,' she said. 'God is calling me. It's a fire in my bones. If I don't go, I'll just burn and die.'

I turned my head. A blouse swung on the pole outside the window.

My hands held the chair so tightly that my fingers turned white. 'I forbid you.'

My daughter left me, went to her room and shut the door behind her. I rubbed the feeling back into my hands.

The next day, when she returned from church, I asked her what she had done. She said, 'Nothing.' She received letters from missionary societies. She stayed out late at night. I asked her where she went. 'Some meeting,' she said. 'Nothing much.' When a man telephoned her, she told me, 'Oh, it was nobody.'

She used to tell me everything. Now she just says, 'Oh nothing.' She used to 'oh nothing' her father; now she has begun to 'oh nothing' me as well.

Two months later, I woke up and she was gone. I went to school to teach the monkeys. The money I earned went into the joint account, and my husband spent it on beer and gambling. When I was home, I cooked meals for two. I did the washing. I put out the washing pole, and the wet clothes danced in the wind. Many nights ago, when she was ten, my daughter begged me to stay. Now I could not ask her to return; God called, and she obeyed.

Today is the Mid-Autumn Festival. It is a year since my daughter's departure. I eat the mooncake I baked for her. Below my balcony, children run across the pavement, in the moonlight. Their lanterns flash, making red shapes of lions, stars, roses on the ground.

My parents never bought lanterns. I made my own lantern, like I do now. My fingers push and pull the wire, forcing it into the right shape. I wrap the red paper around the wire, and place a candle in the middle. Children's laughter floats up to my balcony. Do they know what the lanterns mean?

I taught those monkeys every day so my daughter could be free. But now she is poorer than me. So *gek sim*. She spreads her damaged hands in the photo she sent me. On the postcard she says, 'Built brick kiln for hospital. Hands cut. Performed operation. Local nurse said usually I'm in white coat, so clean, so far from her. When build kiln, hands cut like hers, she feels close to me. God works to create good through all our pain. Very busy. Will write again.'

She lives in Uganda, has so little money, how to survive?

My friends say I'm stupid, they would never let their children work abroad. 'Once you let them go, they never come back.

They say they will visit you, or phone you, but they don't mean it. You'll never see her again.'

My daughter put her arms round me when I bought the Mickey Mouse lantern. 'This is my dream – my best gift.' On Mother's Day, she told me that *I* was her best gift. She sang me a Chinese song she learnt at school: '*In the world, only Mother is good; she who has a mother is like a jewel . . .*'

I don't want her to treat me like her lantern. The lantern made her shout, clap, dance. But when she lost it, she said, 'Forget it, never mind.' She once said I was her best gift. But now that she has left me, what will she say?

I shake my head. My lantern turns, as the wind spins it round. The wind cannot blow out the red light that flashes in the darkness. I raise the red lantern, and pray for her return.

Anil

RIDJAL NOOR

A story from Malaysia, retold by Clare West

Parents always want the best for their children – to give them the best chances in life, to escape from poverty and hunger and despair, to find success, wealth, happiness . . .

The only life Anil knows is one of poverty in a small Indian village. His father and mother are servants of the village headman, and there are no hopes of a better life for Anil, until one hot night in March when a chance suddenly opens . . . but at what price?

On a hot, steamy night in the middle of March, there was a little village where the villagers kept to themselves in small huts, sleeping deeply and dreaming their dreams that rarely came to anything. Probably a new cow for Kuppusamy, the milkman, or a new sewing machine for Rajgopal, who made clothes for all the local people. Housewives dreamed of tomorrow's cooking, and the children dreamed of waking up to another day, and the next, and the next, until it was over as soon as it began. Meanwhile, the streets were completely dark, with no lighting. As the village slept the night away, a little boy in one of the huts was wide awake.

Anil lay awake on his mat, staring up at the roof, where there were many holes in the ceiling. So many that they had to put pots under the various holes every time it rained. But tonight he could only see one hole, because, through it, a small star shone down upon him.

Anil was seven years old, the only son of Ragunathan, the village headman's servant. His mother worked for the headman, too. In a few years, he would also be working for the headman, though he had no knowledge of this. For now, he found the star fascinating. His parents would not even stop for a second to stare at a star. But he did. Because he believed in the magical wonders of life. Because his dreams were bigger than him.

Beside him, on another mat spread on the dusty floor, slept his mother. She wore a faded sari, one of the four that she owned, each as faded as the other. Her blouse was wet under the arms, and rolls of fat were visible around her stomach. Her skin was covered in sweat and a fly hung over it.

Wheee, Anil thought, wheee, the fly slid down the fat.

His mother snored in her sleep, with her head on her right arm. Anil saw the bruise on her shoulder, where Appa, returning home drunk last night, had hit her.

Anil whispered, 'Amma.'

Snooooring.

'Ammaaa . . .'

He badly wanted to pee. He looked up at the bed, where Appa slept. His father was a big strong man, quietly obedient to the headman but often violent to his family. Anil wondered whether to wake him up, but decided he did not need a beating at this time of the night.

He looked back at his mother again. Gently, he reached out with his tiny hand and touched his mother's huge arm, softly shaking her.

'Amma . . .'

Snooooring.

He frowned, then glanced towards the door. He needed to pee, but was afraid of going out into the dark all alone. He might go out and not return. He dared not even think of the reason why he would not return. As if just thinking it was enough to make them come. As if they could read his mind. They. Ghosts.

He sat up on the mat, and looked up at the window. He could see only the dark. Dare he go out?

Then he heard a noise from outside. Feet moving about. Into his eyes came a look of terror. Expecting a ghostly face to appear at the window and send him screaming his head off, still he could not bring himself to look away from the window. If there was something out there, he wanted to be prepared for it. He needed time to scream, time to escape. If there was something out there, he had to know. If there was something out there, he hoped it would not come in here.

'Marimuthu!' a voice half-growled, half-whispered.

Marimuthu? The headman's brother?

Anil stood up very quietly and crept to the window. He was only tall enough to touch the bottom of the window, and he tried to pull himself higher to see what was going on outside, but he couldn't.

'Marimuthu, don't be a coward now! Come here!'

The moon came out from behind a cloud, and Anil saw the large, ghostly tree that grew in front of the hut, the tree with thick creeping plants hanging from its branches.

Even when Anil and his friends played outside in the mornings, they avoided going near the tree. Even in bright daylight, it looked extremely scary. Nagaraj, the madman who sang to himself by the river all day, told them he had once seen the tree wrap its branches around little children who came close and then pull them into its thick crown of leaves, and no one ever saw them again. It was a tree that ate little children.

'Marimuthu!' the voice whispered urgently.

Anil, forgetting for the moment about wanting to pee, could see nothing happening, but he heard the constant movement

Anil turned to his sleeping parents, his mouth opened,
filled with a whisper, but he couldn't find the words.

of feet and the sound of something heavier being dragged on the ground. A rope was thrown over one of the branches of the ghostly tree. It was neatly attached to the branch, and the other end was tied to make a noose, a circle of rope. Anil could see the hands that expertly tied the noose.

He turned to his sleeping parents, his mouth opened, filled with a whisper, but he couldn't find the words. He turned back to the window, his heart beating very fast, very hard. His sweaty hands grabbed the bottom of the window, and he stood on his toes. Still he could not see anyone.

'Help me lift her up!' the same voice whispered.

Two pairs of hands raised a white cloth. Anil's heart stopped for a moment, caught in a shocking discovery. It wasn't a white cloth, it was a woman dressed in white, her long black hair melting into the darkness. They were hanging a woman. Marimuthu and another man. Anil's little body trembled, as a finger of chilling fear crept up his backbone.

They fitted her neck into the noose and let go of her. Suddenly the body shook violently. The woman was still alive! She had been unconscious, but now she had woken, to make a final struggle for her life. It did not last long. After a few moments, the woman's body stopped moving. It swung from side to side on the rope, spinning horribly to face east and then west and then east again. Anil watched, frozen with horror.

He did not know how long it lasted, but after a long while, as the body hung in front of him in silence, he moved away from the window. He moved away to the furthest corner of the hut from the window. He sat, bent over, in the dirt-stained corner, and stayed there for the rest of the night as the other villagers slept and dreamt their little dreams. A small boy, covering his mouth with both hands and silencing the crying that shook his little body, as a star shone above him in the dark sky.

There were no more stars in the morning when Anil woke up. He could hear a lot of noise outside the hut. He saw that he had fallen asleep again, in the corner, curled into a ball. Amma had rolled up her mat and Appa's bed had been pushed against the wall. The sunlight shone in through the window onto the dusty floor. The door had been carelessly left open, and both Amma and Appa were gone. Then he remembered last night.

Looking out of the door, he saw a crowd gathered around the tree. No, don't go there, Anil thought to himself. He saw the noose hanging freely in the air. The body was missing. The tree had pulled it in and swallowed the body. The tree must have spat out the woman's bones, and that's what the unsuspecting villagers must be looking at now. The hanging plants swung carefree in the wind. Any moment now, they would reach out and grab the villagers and eat them all, leaving him alone in the village. Don't go there . . .

He saw his mother talking to some of the other village women. He crept up to her and pulled at her sari. She placed a hand on his head and kept talking. Anil pushed his way deeper into the circle of villagers, where the men stood. Most of them had their arms folded across their chests and heads bent to the ground. Nobody said much; they only kept repeating the same words over and over again. At the centre of the crowd lay the body of the woman. Suddenly Anil was seized by a pair of hands. He turned and saw his father. Appa's eyes were red, but not from sadness; they were always red. Appa held Anil behind him. The little boy looked at the body and held on to his father's shirt.

An old woman sat by the body, holding the dead woman's head on her knees and crying. She was the headman's mother, and she sat on the dusty ground, her mouth open to reveal a toothless mouth. Tears ran down from the sides of her eyes, and she beat her chest and her forehead in sorrow.

A small girl, a little younger than Anil, was crying beside her. Shanti, the woman's daughter. A man knelt on the other side of the body, his face buried in his hands; he was crying loudly.

The woman who had died was his wife.

Marimuthu's wife.

The headman stood behind Marimuthu, calm and unmoving. He finally took a deep breath, and crossed his hands behind his back, a sign to the villagers that he was going to say something important.

'We will bury her body as soon as possible. There is no need to report this. Obviously, my brother's wife chose to end her life, so she killed herself. We are all deeply saddened by this. Why make things worse by telling anyone outside the village?' he said, frowning, his eyes glancing quickly from one face to another as he spoke to the crowd. 'What do you all think?'

Anil's father was one of the first to agree with the headman. The rest of the villagers spoke up, showing their agreement with the headman's wise decision. Anil held his father's shirt tighter.

Marimuthu kept his head to the ground, never looking up once. Anil looked at him, wanting to see the guilt in his eyes.

'Ragunathan, get a bed. We'll take the body away and bury it at once.'

Appa hurried away, leaving Anil standing out in the open, in the centre of the crowd, right in front of the headman, who did not seem to notice him at all.

'Marimuthu, get up, brother. Get yourself together.'

Upon hearing these words from his brother, Marimuthu started crying loudly all over again. The crowd started to become noisy, asking for the reasons why Marimuthu's wife would have wanted to kill herself. The headman stayed silent, angry that his family's personal life had been laid out for public discussion. He heard whispers that the woman had been beaten by Marimuthu. He heard whispers that his family had mistreated her.

Anil suddenly found himself whispering to Marimuthu, 'You killed her. You killed your wife.'

Marimuthu turned sharply to face his accuser, his eyes showing his guilt for one short moment. But then he saw the little boy and pretended to be wrapped in sorrow once again.

The headman's hand came onto Anil's shoulder. Anil looked up at him and repeated his words, 'He did it. I know he did it. I saw it.'

'Come with me, son,' the headman said.

He led the boy out of the crowd, so that none of the villagers could hear Anil's words. Anil's father was coming in their direction, carrying his bed on his shoulder.

'Ragunathan, get someone else to carry on with the burial,' said the headman. 'I want to speak with you.'

Ragunathan dropped the bed and called out to the milkman, Kuppusamy, to replace him. He ran after the headman, who was pulling a confused Anil along beside him. The three of them began to walk to the headman's house.

'I have to talk to you, Ragunathan. I have to talk to you about this son of yours.'

Ragunathan, the uneducated father, unable to read or write, the person with little dreams, the man who was always ready to serve his employer, nodded agreeably.

'You will study hard and be an engineer, or a doctor, or a lawyer. Make this father proud of you. Do you understand? You are very, very lucky to have this chance. You are going to be studying in a big university and becoming someone great one day, you understand? And you'd better not play the fool and mix with bad boys, or I'll come down there and give you a good beating, do you understand?'

Anil looked up at his father and nodded, tears swimming in his eyes. His lower lip trembled.

'Your mother has made these sweets for you. Take them. Don't finish everything on the train. Keep some for later. Be a good boy and don't forget your parents. Remember to write back, understand?'

Anil nodded again, his tears beginning to fall.

'Don't be silly. Men don't cry. You're going into a man's world, you must behave like a man now.'

His father got down from the train and stood outside the window, a hand reaching in to pull Anil towards him and kiss his forehead. The train let out a whistle, announcing its intention to depart in a short while.

'Are you sending me away because I saw him do it?' Anil asked.

Ragunathan was surprised and shocked by the question. He was ashamed of helping the headman to hide the truth about Marimuthu's wife's death. He was also ashamed that he had jumped at the chance to send his son away from the village to receive an education in the town. But this was probably his son's only chance of escape from a life with no hope, a life that Ragunathan was only too familiar with. Was it wrong to sacrifice truth and justice for that?

'Someday you will understand, son, someday you will see that it is for your own good,' his father said. 'It is for the best.'

The train started to move, its tired wheels pushing away from the station. His father held onto his hand and moved along with the train.

'Be a good boy, Anil. Remember your Appa and your Amma. Remember this village,' he cried out as the train gained speed and left the station. Anil put his head outside the window and shouted as loudly as he could, his hands stretched out towards his father.

'Appaaaaa!'

I don't want to go away. I don't want to leave you. Where am I going? How will I know you'll still be here when I come back? Stop this train . . . stop the train!

In the distance, he saw his father fall to his knees, a bent, despairing figure who had just let go of his only son.

I will never forget you, Appa, or forget Amma. I will never forget this village and the evil that it buries today.

Anil sat in his train seat and cried.

A few miles away, in the fields, the villagers stood around the burning body of the woman who had killed herself. Marimuthu, a husband caught in his heartbreaking sorrow, his eyes hidden in his hands, heard the train leaving the village and looked up to see it speeding across the horizon. The heat from the funeral fire changed the shape of the distant train, making it look like a squiggly worm. The headman put his arm around Marimuthu's shoulder. Marimuthu turned to his brother and saw the shadow of a smile on his lips.

He breathed a deep sigh of relief.

My Beloved Charioteer

SHASHI DESHPANDE

A story from India, retold by Clare West

Family relationships are often complicated; and those between mothers and daughters especially can be full of tension, hidden anger, and words left unspoken for too long.

In a household of three women, a widowed grandmother drinks tea with her granddaughter Priti before she goes to school. They talk and laugh together, but quietly, because Aarti, Priti's mother, is still sleeping . . .

I smile as I hear them at last, the sounds I am waiting for. A rush of footsteps, the bang of the bathroom door – I draw in my breath sharply as the sound crashes through the silent house – and, a minute later, another bang. And then, bare feet running towards me.

'You shouldn't bang the doors that way,' I say sternly. 'You might wake Mummy.'

She sits opposite me, with her legs crossed on the low wooden chair, hair untidy, cheeks flushed and warm.

'Oh, she won't wake up for hours yet,' she says cheerfully. 'Have you had your tea, ajji?' Our daily routine. I can never confess to her that I have had a cup an hour earlier. This is her joy, that I wait for her.

'No, I've been waiting for you. Have you brushed your teeth?'

She makes a face. 'I'll do it later,' she says, trying to sound casual.

'You'll do no such thing. Go and brush them at once.'

'Only today, ajji. From tomorrow, I promise, I'll brush them first,' she says persuasively.

'Nothing doing.' I try hard to be firm. But I can't deceive her. She knows I am on her side.

She lowers her voice to a whisper. 'Mummy won't know. She's sleeping.'

Now, of course, she leaves me no choice. I have to be firm. She goes unwillingly. And is back so fast that I have to ask, 'Did you really brush? Properly? Show me.'

'Look.' She is laughing naughtily, and I have to smile back.

'Now tea for me,' she says.

'No,' I say, 'tea for me. Milk for you.'

In the end, as always, we find a solution that pleases both of us, and her tea is a pale brown. Suddenly we realize how loud our voices sound. We look at each other guiltily, thinking of the sleeper, and speak more quietly. Happiness can mean so many things to so many people. For me, it is this. The beginning of a new day with this child. We talk of all kinds of things. But too soon it is time for her to go to school. Bathed and fresh, she sets out.

When she is gone, silence descends on the house. A silence that will not lift until she returns. I had got used to this silence in the last seven years. It had never seemed terrible to me. It was a friendly silence, filled with the ghosts of so many voices in my life – my younger brother, my aunt who loved me when I was a child, my two baby sons who never grew up, and even my daughter Aarti as a child, who seems to have no connection with this thin, bitter woman who now shares the silence with me. But since she came back here, after the death of her husband Madhav, the friendly ghosts have all gone.

It is late before Aarti wakes. I have had my bath, and am halfway through cooking lunch, when I hear her moving about. I take the cooking pot off the fire and put on the tea. By the time tea is ready, she comes into the kitchen. Wordlessly she takes a cup from me, and drinks as if she has been thirsty for hours. Then she pushes the cup back to me, and I pour out some more. I, too, say nothing. Earlier, I used to ask, 'Slept well?' And one day, she put down the cup with a trembling hand and said, 'Slept well? No, I never do that. I haven't slept well since Madhav died. I'll never sleep well again all my life. I have to take something every night so that I can close my eyes for a few hours. Now, never ask me again if I slept well.'

Nine months I carried this daughter of mine in my body. I felt within me every beat of her heart, every movement of her limbs. But I knew that my pains and shocks could never hurt her, she was so well protected. Even now, she is protected from my pains. Even now, I have no protection against her pains. My suffering is of no use. I cannot help her. I can only be clumsy and make things worse.

'Why didn't you let me know earlier?' she asked me angrily, when she came home after her father's death.

'Don't tell Aarti yet,' he had told me, 'I don't want to frighten her. Especially not now.'

Habits of obedience die harder than any other. I had not dared to inform Aarti. And the next day he had another attack and died instantly. Three months later Priti was born. She never saw her grandfather.

'Who is that, ajji?' she asked me once, seeing his photo.

'Your grandfather, Priti.'

'My grandfather,' she said thoughtfully. 'And what was he of yours?'

What was he of mine? The innocent question released a flood of feelings within me. 'My husband,' I said at last, bluntly.

As I get on with cooking lunch, I wonder whether today Aarti will like what I am cooking. Whether she will enjoy her food and eat well. I know she will not, but the hope is always in me. Just as I hope that one day she will talk and laugh again. But on the day when she had laughed, her laughter too loud for the quiet house, she had frightened me. 'What is it?' I asked her, wondering whether to smile, to laugh, to respond in some way.

'Look at us! A pair of widows.'

Widows . . . I remember my mother, who was one. She had a shaven head, wore only coarse red saris and no jewellery all her life after my father's death. And I think of Aarti, who for days forgets to brush her hair, or even wash. And then, one day, dresses in her best and wears flowers in her hair. But it is Aarti whose face has the dried-up look of a desert.

Life has been cruel to her. It was her father whom she loved, and he died, while I live. It was her husband whom she loved even more than the child, and it was he who died, while Priti is left to her.

Children are more sensitive than we think. They understand so many things we think they don't. Otherwise why would she have said one day to me, 'Ajji, can I sleep in your room at night?'

I am old and grey and have lost all that I loved in life except these two persons, but at her words, my heart jumped in happiness. However, I held back my joy and asked her, 'Why, Priti?'

*I am old and grey and have lost all that I loved in life
except these two persons.*

'I'd like to. You can tell me stories at night. And there are so many things I suddenly remember at night and want to tell you. And—'

'But Mummy is with you.'

The child's face looked sad. 'But, ajji, if I try to talk to her, she says, "Go to sleep, Priti, and don't bother me." And she never sleeps at all, she just reads and smokes. And I don't like that smell.'

'Quiet, Priti,' I said, suddenly afraid that her high, clear voice might be overheard. Yes, Aarti smokes all the time now. When I was a child, it was considered wrong even for a man to smoke. But today, I would not mind my daughter smoking if I thought it brought her happiness. But it doesn't. The smoke she creates is full of bitterness. And I cannot help her. I can only try to look after her body. Such a small thing to do, but even in that I fail. She is thin and delicate-looking. Most of the time she just goes round in an old dress, her hair tied up with a rubber band. One day Priti saw an old photo of her and said sadly, 'My Mummy was so pretty, wasn't she, ajji?'

The little girl's pride in her mother made me angry with Aarti. She seems like a child who is sulking because she doesn't have what she wants. I want to ask her, has anyone promised us happiness for a lifetime?

'Why don't you go out?' I asked her once.

'Where?' she replied. 'There is nowhere I want to go. Everywhere, I see couples. I can't bear to see them. I could murder them when I see them talking and laughing.'

This talk amazes me. I cannot understand her. My niece once told me of something she had read in an American magazine. About children of eleven, twelve, thirteen, and fourteen who are guilty of horribly violent crimes – often for no reason. And I wondered at the time, what kind of parents can they be who give birth to such monsters? Now I know better. The accident of birth can be cruelly deceiving. We think that our children are our own, that we know them. But often, they are strangers to us. Still, we can never escape the responsibility of being parents. If my daughter is so empty that she can hate people who are happy, the fault is, to some extent, mine.

These bitter thoughts do not often occupy me. I have my work in the house. The quiet routine of my day brings calm to my soul. Now that the child is with me, the day is full of meaning. I wait, as eager as a child myself, for her to return from school. When she has a holiday, I don't know who is happier, she or I. But when she, *my* daughter and *her* mother, comes to us, we feel guilty and hide our happiness.

'Do you remember your father?' Aarti asked her harshly one day.

'Father?' There was a moment's hesitation. 'Of course, I remember.'

'I don't think you do. You never speak of him.'

The child stared at her with a frightened face, feeling guilty but not knowing why. And when Aarti left us, she burst out crying and held me tightly. I was full of pity, not for her, but for Aarti, who could turn happiness into a wrong. But I can say nothing to her. She has never shared anything with me, and now she hides her sorrow like a dog its bone. She guards it jealously and will not let me approach. And I have kept my distance. It was only in my imagination that I held her in my arms when she was a child, only in my imagination that I shared her happiness and secrets when she was a young girl. And now I help her to bear her sorrow in the same way. 'Look,' I tell myself I will say to her, pouring some water into my cupped palms. 'Look,' I will say as the water falls through my fingers, leaving nothing. 'You cannot hold on. You will have to let it go.'

But I know I'm deceiving myself. I have no courage to speak. I am only a foolish woman who has never known how to win anyone's love. Priti's love – that is a gift of heaven, it is a ray of sunshine that lights up the dark corners of my life. For Aarti, it was always her father. Even now, she spends the whole afternoon in what was his room. It is seven years since he died, but the room is unchanged. I have kept everything as it was. I dust and clean it carefully. But strangely, in spite of this, it looks as if no one cares about it. Priti sometimes looks the same. She is well-fed and well-dressed, but even so, there is an uncared-for look in her eyes at times, which fills me with sadness.

Now I can hear Aarti moving round in his room. Even after his death, he can give her something I can't. The thought hurts. Hurts? It's like having salt rubbed into an open wound. Suddenly it is unbearable and I go and open the door of his room. She is sitting on his chair, her feet on his table, smoking and staring at nothing. She hears me and turns round quickly – I have never disturbed her until now – and with the movement of her feet she knocks down his photograph which stood on the table. Now it lies on the floor, face down. She rushes to pick it up. The glass has cracked, and long pieces of glass lie on the floor. She looks up at me. 'I'm sorry, mother, I'm sorry.' I stare down at the photograph and say nothing. 'I'm sorry,' she repeats. 'Don't look like that. I'll get it fixed tomorrow. I promise I'll do it.'

'No, don't!' My voice sounds hard and she looks at me in surprise. 'I don't care if it's broken. I never want to see it again.'

She looks up at me, amazed, frightened. 'What's wrong with you? What's happened to you?'

'Nothing. I'm all right. But I don't want it. Let it go.'

'What are you saying? What is it?'

'Let it go, let it go,' I repeat. We are speaking in whispers. Can he hear us? Can he hear me?

'I don't understand you. Let what go? He is my father.' She is still kneeling there on the floor, holding the photograph in her two hands.

'Yes, your father. But what was he to me? The day he died, I let him go. Like that.' Now I make the movement I had imagined – putting my hands together like a cup and then separating them. She stares at my hands with fascinated eyes. 'And there was nothing left. Nothing.'

'But I – I am his daughter. And yours. Am I nothing? Am I?' She is breathing fast, her eyes hot and angry.

'What are you then?' I ask her. 'You are just smoke and a bit of ash – like those cigarettes you smoke. Like my married life.' Pain lays its claws on her face. But I force myself to go on. What have I to lose? Nothing. Only the child's love. And this cannot destroy that. In fact, I have a feeling that she is with me now, giving me strength for the battle, encouraging me to fight. My beloved charioteer, my guide – like Lord Krishna was to Arjuna before the battle of Kurukshetra.

'He was your father,' I go on, 'but what was he of mine? I lived with him for twenty-five years. I know he didn't like stones in his rice. I know he liked his tea boiling hot and his bathwater only just warm. I know he didn't like tears. And so, when your baby brothers died, I cried alone and in secret. I combed my hair before he woke up because he didn't like to see women with loosened hair. And once a year he bought me two saris, always colours that I hated. But he never asked me and I never told him. And at night—'

She is still kneeling on the floor, holding the photograph, her hair falling about her face. 'Don't!' she cries. 'Don't tell me! Don't!' With each word she bangs the photograph and the glass breaks again and again. Now he is openly on view to both of us. But there is no pity in me. It is not the dead who need your sympathy – it is the living.

'I don't want to hear,' she says.

How innocent she is in spite of her age, her education, her books, her marriage and her child who can still be hurt by knowledge. It reminds me of the day I realized she had grown up, and I tried to explain. She cried out then in the same way, 'Don't tell me. Don't!' This is another kind of growing up, when you learn to see your parents as people.

'At night,' I go on, pitiless, 'I scarcely dared to breathe, I was so terrified of disturbing him. And once – I don't know how I had the courage – I asked whether I could sleep in another room. But the next day, his mother, your grandmother, told me very plainly about a wife's duties. I must always be available. So I slept there, afraid to get up for a glass of water, scared even to cough. When he wanted me, he said, "Come here." And I went. And when he finished, if I didn't get out of his bed fast enough, he said, "You can go." And I went.' I know these things should not be said to her, his daughter and mine. But I am like a river in flood. I have no control over myself.

'And one day when you were here – you and Madhav – I heard you both laughing and talking in your room. And I stood outside and wondered, what could you be talking about? I felt like I did when I was a child, unable to read, looking at a book. Until then, I had hoped that one day he would say he was pleased with me. That day, I knew it would never happen. I would always be outside the room. I would never know what goes on inside. And that day, I envied you, my own daughter. You hear me, Aarti? I envied you. And when he died, I felt like Priti does when school is over and the bell rings. You understand, Aarti? You understand?'

Why am I also crying? We look at each other. She looks at me as if she has never seen me before. Then, with a sudden movement, she jumps up and stares angrily at me. Whose is the victory? Whose? I have made her look at me. But what if she does not like what she sees? My heart shrinks at the thought. And as she moves backwards and starts running away from the room, from me, I realize what I have done. And then I hear the cry, 'Ajji, I'm home. Where are you?'

'Here,' I call back loudly. 'I'm here.'

A Dream of China

OVIDIA YU

A story from Singapore, retold by Clare West

Few people understand the pain of exile if they have not experienced it – when the heart aches to breathe the air, to gaze at the mountains, to walk the streets of the place called 'home'.

A daughter observes the pain of exile in her father, still dreaming of home in China after fifty happy years in Singapore. But dreams are made of wishes and hopes; reality can be deeply disappointing, as his daughter discovers . . .

He was a grey old man in old worn clothes, and he spoke with the crossness of one who has known for years that he is unlucky in life. Could I get him out of China? he asked. I thought of my modern little flat and my husband and babies, and I couldn't imagine the man sleeping on our Italian leather sofa. I want to see your father again, the grey old man unwisely said. That decided the matter. I did not want him to see my father again. If I had anything to do with it, he would never see my father again. The sad, dishonest eyes lost the watery hold they had gained on my sympathy. My mind stopped wondering where an extra bed could be fitted, and began to search for a polite way to say 'No'.

My father is a good man. My mother – his second wife – died soon after I was born, and my father retired in order to have the time to bring me up. Until then, he had been a scientist at the University of Singapore. He still produced an occasional scientific article in between teaching me the right way to hold a Chinese writing brush and telling me stories. As I grew up and he grew older, his stories were more and more often about China.

China was the most beautiful of beautiful countries, where he had spent his youth. After fifty years in Singapore, 'home' for him was still Szechuan, in south-west China.

My elder sisters and brother, all children of his first marriage and many years older than me, warned me, 'Whenever he sees anything particularly beautiful, he says that's how it is in China. You mustn't believe all of it, you know!'

They were sorry for me, a child living with an old man who told the same stories over and over again. But children love repetition. I began to dream dreams of China too. I, who was born countless miles from China on this island of Singapore. I dreamed of the strange mountains and calm waters. I dreamed of the magic creatures. In China there were spirits in the trees and the animals. All this was much more interesting than the Western stories of magic, with their over-colourful pictures of white people with wings. More interesting, too, than daily life in Singapore. Here, the closest thing to magic was the primary school toilet where a ghost was supposed to live.

But there was one thing about China that made my father feel extremely guilty. Because of that, he had decided that he would die in exile, never to return.

After the Second World War, when the Japanese gave up Singapore and left China, my father and his younger brother had a choice. They could stay in Singapore or they could return to build a new China. In their youth – and they were still young then – the brothers had believed in the revolution. Against their father's wishes, both had left home to join the army, which was fighting to bring new life to the rotten, dying nation they loved. At home, they had seen China through the eyes of the fortunate, as sons of a wealthy man. In the army, and disinherited by their father, they saw their country differently – wild and bruised, but still beautiful. It is hard to understand the appeal of a beautiful and suffering country, but it existed in China then.

At that time, my father had a steady income from teaching, in Singapore. He had his wife and my eldest sister, who was already born. He chose to stay in Singapore. It was this decision that, in later years, he considered his most cowardly act. His younger brother returned to China to help rebuild the country after the war. My father remained in Singapore.

He missed China very much. He saw his act of selfishness reflected in the shallowness of the lives his university students led. All they did was study. If they did dream, it was of having a reliable job and owning a car. Most of his students were Chinese, but they did not have the determination they should have. That determination which his younger brother had and he lacked!

My elder sisters and brother laughed at him. 'Young Singaporeans are practical,' my third sister used to say. 'Do you want them to start a revolution when they don't see anything wrong with the country?' And my brother would ask, 'What do you think is wrong with Singapore?' My father could see only one thing wrong with Singapore, but that one thing counted for more than anything else: Singapore was not China. He had failed to return to China as his brother had. His younger brother had done right and he had done wrong. He was too overcome by shame to return later, when he was older.

'But lots of people go round China on the tours,' my brother tried to persuade him. 'They have special tours just for old people. You're always talking about going back. Why don't you go now? You may not have many years left, you know. I'll pay for the trip, of course. There's a tour group leaving in the second week of June. Why don't you let me get you a place on that one?'

My brother is not easy to resist, but my father resisted him. He felt he did not deserve to see China again, although he wanted to very much. Instead, he wrote poems in Chinese about living in exile, and he tried to live as he felt a true Chinese would.

He was Westernized to a certain extent and did not demand unquestioning obedience from his children. Being Chinese, for him, meant remaining calm at all times, respecting the servants' feelings, and never thinking about financial gain.

My father sympathized with his second daughter's son, whose name was Golden Dragon. The boy was trying to find out more about his father's family, his identity as a human being. 'Without the experience of your ancestors before you, it is hard to build a strong future,' my father said to Golden Dragon. We knew he was thinking not only of his grandson, but of his children who had never seen the graves of their ancestors in Szechuan.

The years passed. I discovered that not everyone viewed China as my father did. The Red Guards took over all of China, and Chinese people living overseas sent money, woollen clothes, and pity to those left behind. This made my father feel even worse, as he lived in comfort away from his country instead of suffering with her.

I learnt more about my father's feelings after I married. He told my husband, whose name was Heavenly Wisdom, things he felt a girl should not hear. My husband, who was not so sensitive, passed them on to me.

It was not only shame for ignoring the call of his country that had kept my father from China all these years, Heavenly Wisdom said. There was also the letter which his brother had written to him, when my father had reconsidered and spoken of returning to China only months after his brother. (Heavenly Wisdom guessed that the younger brother had taken over their dead father's house and the remaining wealth of the family. If my father returned, all would have to be given up to him, as he was the elder son.) The letter said my father should not return if he cared about the family at all. He had married without their parents' agreement, and his wife was used to city life in Singapore. Would his wife miss Singapore and want to return, causing their lands to be sold to support her in luxury? My father could not say no with certainty. He felt shame that his younger brother was wiser than him in such matters. He decided not to displace such a dutiful son by returning himself.

'I didn't know he ever meant to go back to China,' I said to my husband, surprised. 'He never told me that.'

'That was in 1946, long before your time,' Heavenly Wisdom said absently. 'Anyway, after the Red Guards took over, there was no question of going back.'

'He didn't go back just because of a letter from his brother? I would have gone back anyway, and claimed everything that was mine by right!'

'Living in China under the Red Guards would have been no joke. It's a good thing your father didn't go back.'

'But he could have gone back to China and taken everything

and come back to Singapore, and then he would be rich as well as free,' I argued.

My husband shook his head mildly. 'If he had gone back to China, he would never have left again. Baby One is eating my black socks.' He always referred to our sons as Baby One and Baby Two. When they ate socks and other things, he watched them with scientific interest, but did nothing to prevent them. For that reason, in the early years of our marriage, I had little time to think about my father and his brother in China.

My father did not allow age to weaken his health or cut down his activities. After I married, he moved to a place called Pasir Ris, where he spent his days looking after his plants, writing poems about exile and drinking tiger bone wine. He had never given up his interest in Chinese writing. Often my husband and I took the babies on the long drive up to Pasir Ris, where their grandfather taught their little hands to hold the Chinese brush in the correct way and told them stories about China. Sometimes my father and my husband walked along the beach barefoot, playing a scientific game, which involved identifying sea creatures and giving their scientific names.

As these were serious scientific expeditions, the babies and I were never allowed to go with them, and it was during one of the expeditions that I discovered some of my father's poems while cleaning his study room. My father never minded me reading his poems. I found my favourite one:

> Lovely silent carp
> Circling my ornamental pond
> Like a wise thought.
> Is all water your element
> Or do you dream of wide brimming rivers
> As I have a dream of home?

Surely my father was content in Singapore after all these years? But it was still an ornamental pond and not the wide brimming river. Not home. My father's writing made me miss the China I had never known. Now, that was beautiful poetry. It stirred up your feelings, as well as pleasing the ear and the eye.

At the back of the book of poems, there was a packet of letters I had not seen before. They were all from the wife of my father's younger brother, and they were all letters asking for money to be sent.

'Did you send them money?' I asked my father when he and my husband returned.

'Yes, I believe I did,' he said. He took the letters from me and looked at them, vaguely puzzled.

'More money than he should have. It's a good thing I'm not the sort of man to marry for wealth!' my husband said cheerfully. I could tell he had won their scientific game that day.

'I would not have given my daughter away to such a man!' my father replied, pretending to be very proud.

'But why were they always asking for money? After all, my uncle returned to build a new China. Don't they treat him well there? And why does my uncle's wife write instead of him writing to you himself?'

One of my babies began to cry for me. Heavenly Wisdom went off to pick him up, and through the doorway I saw him trying to discover whether babies ate grass. My babies did not, and they both began to cry very loudly. For that reason, I did not hear my father's reply. My father did not seem to want to discuss the matter again after that, and I was left to wonder.

Then I was offered a chance to go to China. It was a tour for university students. Young Singaporeans could read and write beautifully correct Chinese, but were awkward when it came to conversation. I was invited to go on the tour because my spoken Chinese was so good, and because it was thought I knew something about China, being my father's daughter. It was my opportunity, at last, to see the land of my people.

I wanted to go on the tour very much, but it was not my place to say anything. So I waited, trying to look patient, as my husband thought about it. He did not have much enthusiasm for China. His parents had never spoken to him of China, except of their relief to have left in time. To him, the old China had been a country of rottenness and suffering, where whole families starved to death and daughters were sold. The new China had only slightly more appeal for him. I did not expect him to give permission for me to leave him and the babies for such a trip.

'You may go if you wish,' he said in the end.

'They only pay half the expenses, so you will have to pay the other half,' I reminded him.

'Do you doubt I can do that?' Heavenly Wisdom asked drily. So it was agreed, and I went to China for two weeks.

It is not my intention to describe China. I am writing of my family – my father and his younger brother.

Something I had set myself to achieve in China was to visit my father's home town, where my uncle and his wife still lived. There were few other relations left alive. The tour brought us within two hours of my destination. Apparently, two hours' travel is a huge distance to most people in China, where they often calculate distance by bicycle rather than by car. However, I was able to rent a car, and two students and a guide came with me. As we travelled through farmland and small towns, I could not imagine my father there.

True, there was much beauty in China. On a boat trip the day before, we had all been amazed by the breathtaking loveliness of the river, nearby mountains with their caves of ice, and distant hills dreamy and purple in their vagueness. It seemed a journey back through time into an age of timelessness.

But seeing the Chinese people, I felt glad I was a tourist. China spoke to my mind. The idea that this country was where my ancestors came from warmed and stirred me. However, China had nothing to say to my spirit. My spirit felt as foreign here as I did, and only really felt at home in a city full of purpose and enterprise, shining like a diamond in the modern world. That was where I truly belonged, among glass-fronted office blocks reaching to the sky. When I finally met my uncle, I felt like a visitor to a strange country, not a returning exile.

I saw he had the face of my father. He was thin, with skin like old leather. He spat noisily. When I asked if he had any message for my father, he said, 'Tell him to send money.'

I stayed to have dinner with my aunt and uncle, while the students and guide ate at the foreigners-only hotel where we were going to spend the night. I tried to remember everything I could. My father would take delight in every detail I could give him.

There were just two rooms, with black-and-white photos and a few books. The food was simple and well prepared. All through the meal my uncle swore continuously at his wife and at my father. My father must have known it would come to this, he said. That was why he had not returned. He had always been the clever one. Why had my father not warned him? He had let his brother walk right into it! If my father had only given him a word of warning, he would now be in Singapore living in luxury, not being miserable and badly treated in this hole, married to this misery of a wife who deserved to be dead.

I felt sorry for him. After all, he had the face of my father. I thought of my father, calm and happy in his garden, making scientific notes in his study room, and was thankful that circumstances had kept him away from China.

Surely my father sent him money? I asked, knowing that he did. My uncle replied loudly that he had never asked for any, then he firmly denied getting any money from my father, and finally he claimed he didn't get enough money from my father. During this confusing reply, my aunt softly said, 'Yes, your father sends money. He is too good to us. Your uncle knows but will not admit it. Too proud.'

I did not try any further remarks. My aunt nervously urged me to take more food, while my uncle continued his muttered swearing and self-pity.

I gave my uncle the money my father had given me for him, and a cassette-recorder and camera. My uncle complained because my father had not remembered to send cigarettes and because only one roll of film came with the camera. What good would the camera be to him after that? He could not afford more film himself, surely I could see that! But my aunt asked me to thank my father. They might sell the camera, she said. It would keep them going well for some time. As my uncle stood there, inspecting the camera and tape-recorder and complaining under his breath, my aunt and I washed the dinner bowls together.

'He got some of my relations into trouble,' she told me in a low voice. 'Now my family won't have anything to do with us. Neither will his family. I don't blame them. He betrayed his own cousin on his mother's side. The village children shout names at him and their parents encourage them. He will not work. He will not even ask for money. I have to do that.' She sighed softly; the hair falling untidily on to her face was yellow-white. 'Your father always sends money when I ask for it, always a little more than I ask for. He is a good man.'

'Yes,' I agreed.

We talked quietly about different relations and what they were doing. Soon my uncle announced he was going to walk me to the hotel. I bowed goodbye to my aunt. She told me to give their thanks and best wishes to my family, especially my father.

The October night was cold. There were yellow pools of street light with great areas of darkness between them. We walked from pool to pool in silence. Finally we reached the hotel.

'We leave early tomorrow,' I said awkwardly. 'I suppose I won't see you again on this visit.'

The man who was my father's brother looked hungrily past me at the gate of the hotel gardens.

'The only time we get to go inside is if a foreigner invites us in as guests,' he said pointedly. 'There is a bar where you can buy me a drink. It's been years since I was invited to have a drink here.'

'Why don't you come in for a drink?' I felt obliged to say. He accepted with child-like excitement, breathing hard in his eagerness as I held the gate open and the gatekeeper waved us both in, without checking identification.

With great grandness, my uncle ordered orange drinks from the waiter. He criticized the glasses as dirty when the drinks arrived, and insisted on new ones. To this man my father had trusted the good name of his family – a family now far apart

*There were yellow pools of street light with great areas of darkness
between them. We walked from pool to pool in silence.*

and in disharmony. Could my father live with that, I wondered? One thing that had calmed his spirit in the long years of exile was the thought that he had done right in leaving everything to his brother, who was a better person than he was. I stared at the man swallowing flat orange juice and felt a growing dislike. My father had made a mistake there! But this man had done me a great service by his greed. He had kept my father in Singapore. For that, I owed him a lot.

Finally, he let me walk him back to the gate. Just inside the wall, he turned and took one of my hands in both of his and cried. Tears dropped off his chin. I didn't know what to say, wishing with all my heart I had not come to China, and not stirred up such feelings in this miserable failure of a man.

When he calmed down, I said, 'We will send you things from Singapore.'

'Can you get me out of China?' he asked. 'I want to come back to Singapore. Just me, one person. No wife.'

Where would he live in Singapore? Not with my father. There was little room in Pasir Ris. There was little room in our flat too. He couldn't sleep on the sofa! And what about his wife, alone in China?

'I want to see your father again,' the man said. An angry, cheated look had come back into his eyes. He obviously felt that my father owed him a lot.

No. I would not do this to my father. I wanted to return to Singapore to tell him my uncle was well in China. That he was too busy (not too lazy) to write himself. My father could then breathe easily, believe he had done a good thing, and enjoy in his old age the benefits of the good life he had lived and the children he had brought up. This man must not be allowed to come and spoil everything!

'Don't leave me to die here, I have not long to live. I want to get out. Can you get me out?'

'We will talk of getting you out when my father has left this world,' I said. I would never tell my father about this.

He understood. He thanked me and walked away, weighed down by hopelessness and his bad nature. I watched him through the gate. A grey old man in old worn clothes wandering from pool to pool of yellow light. It was as though he was the spirit of China, now broken and leaving me. Leaving me for ever, because I could tell he would not outlive my father. If his wife did, I promised myself I would take care of her.

My father's China no longer exists, except in him and in other men who try to live true to the dream of China in their hearts. I returned to Singapore, feeling no connection with the China I saw, but no less eager to listen to my father's stories of the most beautiful of all beautiful lands. A country is only as good as its men. My father is a good man . . . whichever country can claim him as its own.

Lily

NORA ADAM

A story from Malaysia, retold by Clare West

Marriages fail for all kinds of reasons, and the blame might be with the man, or the woman, or with both. But the ones who suffer most from a failed marriage are often the children. They get caught up in the war between their parents, and are even used as weapons in that war.

Adam sits on the bus, holding a huge pink teddy bear, and thinking about the turning points in his life . . .

There were certain events in Adam's life that clearly marked the beginning of a new turning point for him.

His first bicycle.

The day he scored the winning goal for his regional team, and slept with a girl for the first time that same night.

The moment the first woman he fell in love with agreed to be his wife.

The day he became a father.

The night he began to sleep with someone who was not his wife.

He thought about the latest turning point in his life as he sat on the bus, holding the oversized pink teddy bear tightly and ignoring the looks he was getting from the other passengers. The bear had been too big to fit into his bag, and anyway, he didn't want it to be squashed. So he carried it proudly, pretending not to notice the laughs and glances thrown his way, even as his arms were aching from the damp heat and the awkwardness of the large toy. Two more hours and it would all be worth it, he thought. Two more hours added to the six long months that he hadn't seen Lily. He wondered how much a child could grow in half a year. Would he still recognize her? This thought continued to worry him as the heat and the steady movement of the bus sent him into an uneasy sleep.

'Why didn't you call me last night?' she had complained as he whispered hello.

Adam was outside on the balcony. He took a long pull at his cigarette and looked over his shoulder towards the kitchen as he blew the smoke out through his nose.

'Sorry, I didn't have time,' he explained. 'My daughter was sick and we were up all night taking care of her.' He wondered if the people in the apartment below could hear him. Who cares? he thought, it's not as if they knew him or Lisa.

Silence on the other side. Nadia being moody again.

'Baby, I'm calling you now, aren't I?' he said. 'It was the first chance I got.'

Inside the apartment, he could hear the sound of chicken being fried as Lisa prepared dinner. Lily had been given some medicine, and was finally asleep and quiet.

'Yes, it's always whenever the time is convenient for you. You don't really care about me, what I might be going through. It's all about when you're free, when you have the time to call. I have a timetable too, you know!' cried Nadia.

God, not this again, he sighed. I already get enough complaining from my wife without having to put up with it from Nadia as well.

'Look, you know my situation. I did call you as soon as I could. You can't expect me to drop everything and come running to you whenever you want. I have responsibilities, for God's sake!'

As soon as the words came out, he knew they were a mistake. Nadia was half crying and half laughing in shocked amazement as she spat out his own words back at him.

'I have responsibilities! I have responsibilities?! Who do you think you are, trying to sound like a good husband and father? Don't forget, family man, it's me you're sleeping with!' she shouted.

She had a point, Adam admitted to himself. 'Nadia, OK, calm down. I'm sorry, OK? I'm just a little tired right now. I haven't slept in nearly two days. I'll see you after work tomorrow, OK?'

Silence again before Nadia finally gave in.

'Hmmm,' she said, but he knew that meant that everything was fine again between them. That was the one thing he could depend on. In the end, Nadia always gave in.

'Adam?' Lisa called out from the kitchen. She was a very efficient cook.

'I've got to go, baby. Call you tomorrow, OK?' He quickly slipped the cell phone into his back pocket, put out the cigarette and opened the balcony door.

'Dinner,' Lisa announced as Adam re-entered the apartment and walked towards her.

The bus braked suddenly, waking Adam as his head hit the back of the seat in front of him. He cried out in pain, then quickly grabbed the teddy bear before it fell on the dirty floor of the bus.

'Lucky for you, you brought along your bear for comfort,' said the man sitting next to him, laughing unpleasantly.

Adam ignored him and stared out of the window, rubbing the sleep from his eyes. Not far now. He recognized some of the old shops of the small town they were passing. He remembered the first time he saw the grey-white fronts of these buildings, all those years ago when he had gone to ask Lisa's parents for her hand in marriage. It felt almost like a lifetime ago. Here he was again, full circle, back to where he and Lisa started, his past joy and present pain meeting with a bump. He gave a heavy sigh and moved the teddy bear to a more comfortable position.

Lisa had finally called back after the many, many calls he made. He had begged for forgiveness, claiming that Nadia was only a moment of madness, and lying that it was just that one time, the one time Lisa caught them. He remembered that disastrous moment. Talk about coincidences! Of all days, Lisa just happened to leave her cell phone at home. And of all the places in the largest city in the country, Lisa's car just happened to break down right outside the dark little restaurant where he and Nadia used to meet before going upstairs to her flat on the first floor. A dusty, poorly lit restaurant, so very unlike the type of place that Lisa would go to, except on the unfortunate day that she needed to use the nearest phone to call for breakdown assistance.

When he saw her walk in and turn her head towards them, he was so shocked that he failed to withdraw his hand from its loving hold on Nadia. He was frozen in his seat, as Lisa's face showed doubt, denial, shock, anger, and hurt. Tears spilling down her face, she let out a pitiful cry and spun round towards the door. She almost tripped in her hurry to get away, to escape to a view that was not of her husband lovingly touching another woman. Outside, she had stopped a taxi which, mercifully, took her away faster and faster from the sight that had torn out her heart.

By the time Adam got home, Lisa and Lily were gone. Lisa had grabbed whatever she could and run away to the safety of her sister's home. In an instant, his two worlds had come crashing down, and none of their inhabitants would ever fully recover.

He got off the bus and stood on the roadside, teddy bear in one hand, a bag of clothes in the other. There were no taxis or public buses in sight. It would be a three-kilometre walk in the full heat of the sun to get to the house. He held the bear more firmly, took out the address again and started walking.

Not surprisingly, Lisa got a divorce and was allowed to keep Lily. As far as the courts were concerned, she was the perfect wife and mother; she was even a socially aware teacher, who gave her less fortunate students free lessons after school. Adam and his relationship with Nadia were blamed for the failure of the marriage, so it was hard for him to even get visiting rights. It was months before he saw Lily again. Even then it was at Lisa's sister's house, where all eyes watched him accusingly as he tried to talk to his daughter. Probably because of the unfriendly atmosphere, or because she hadn't seen him in a while, Lily behaved shyly around him, responding to him only after much encouragement, until finally she ran and hid behind her mother.

Adam had wanted to ask there and then when he could come and see Lily again. But the words stuck in his throat as he saw the look of hurt, hatred, and bitterness flashing in Lisa's eyes – the same look he had seen at the restaurant. It was pointless to even tell her that he and Nadia were history. He knew Lisa would not forgive him and would certainly never take him back. So he avoided any argument, choosing instead to phone afterwards to arrange for the next visit. But the next time was harder to arrange. Lisa was often busy with work or Lily had art class or swimming or was out with her grandparents. He supposed he deserved it, but he still missed his daughter.

Then one day Lisa left a message, telling him that she was moving to her parents' hometown. She had been transferred to a school there, and she and Lily were leaving in a few days. He tried phoning her back many times but couldn't reach her. He knew that any attempt to contact her through her sister would be useless. He felt anxious and helpless. Luckily for him, Lisa did call back eventually. She and Lily had now moved, and if he wanted, he could come and see Lily, but he would have to find a place to stay overnight. Adam accepted immediately and took the first bus there, to see his daughter.

A car stopped and the driver offered to take him as far as the town, so he arrived at the house earlier than expected. Through the trees surrounding the house, he heard screams of laughter. He soon saw Lisa spinning Lily around and around in the front yard as they both laughed wildly. His heart ached with love. Love and regret. He walked slowly towards them, unwilling to disturb their fun but wanting so much to hold his daughter once more. But he waited a moment longer. It had been so long since he last saw Lisa smile. Then Lily turned her head towards him, inheriting the movement from her mother, and paused in her laughter. Lisa stopped laughing too, though she kept smiling as she turned to share her daughter's view. The moment their eyes met, Lisa's smile dropped instantly and the guarded look in her eyes returned. She put Lily down and held her hand as they walked towards him.

'Hi,' he said, 'sorry I'm early.'

Lisa nodded. The three of them stood looking at each other in silence. It was suddenly awkward. Lily's eyes were on the teddy bear, and Adam suddenly felt hugely grateful for the fact that he had brought it, despite all the unpleasantness of the bus journey. He knelt down in front of Lily and said,

'This is for you.'

Lily looked up at her mother, who nodded her permission and gently pushed Lily's hand towards the toy bear.

Giving a shy smile, Lily took the bear from Adam and held it tightly in her arms, her cheeks a rosy pink. Adam's heart swelled with so much love and happiness, as he saw his daughter's shining eyes and her excitement with her new toy.

Then she said in a soft innocent voice, ever so politely, 'Thank you, *Uncle.*'

And Adam felt his heart break into a million tiny pieces.

A Child is Born

NIRUPAMA SUBRAMANIAN

A story from India, retold by Clare West

'The birth of a boy is welcomed with shouts of joy, but when a girl is born, the neighbours say nothing,' so the old saying goes. Poor families in many countries prefer boy babies. Sons stay at home and farm the family's land to support their ageing parents, but daughters . . . daughters are expensive to marry, and then they leave home to join their husbands' families.

In a poor Indian village a family waits for the birth of a child . . .

It was a hot, dull night in May, the air was heavy as a blanket and the moonless sky hung like a great snake's head over the small mud hut. A man sat outside the hut, his hands holding his bony knees, looking like a clumsy question mark. He was waiting.

Inside the hut, his wife arched her back in pain as the midwife's fingers pushed this way and that at her swollen stomach. His mother watched, her face expressionless. Soon, the midwife pulled out a tiny, crying baby.

'Girl,' she muttered.

The man outside the hut swore loudly. His mother hit her forehead with her open hand and sighed. The young midwife sank back on the hard mud floor and tried not to feel anything.

If the news had been different, she might have received a new sari or a few coins. Instead, she quickly finished her work, and crept away into the night, like a criminal.

The man's mother finally spoke. 'You know what has to be done.'

The woman who had just become a mother knew what had to be done. She knew the women in the village did it in many ways. Some used poisonous plants. Others rolled a sari into a tight ball, so the baby could not breathe. Others offered their baby to the river goddess. She wished her own mother had done it years ago. Then she would not have seen her parents, already heavily in debt, sell their animals and belongings to pay for her own marriage – and a marriage to a poor farmer, who already had debts of his own. Girls, she had been told since childhood, brought only tears and unhappiness to others, and into their own miserable lives. She knew that a son, who carried on the family name and promised a safe passage to heaven, made his parents live for ever.

Her husband's mother leaned over to take the baby, but the woman said, 'I will do it.' She wrapped the baby in an old cloth, and forced some strength into her aching body. It was a long way to the river. She walked through the solid blackness, tripping over the stones, until she heard the steady sound of the waters. The river seemed peaceful, with no sign of the secrets and small bodies that lay within it.

The bundle in her arms moved, and although she had promised herself not to look at its face, the woman found herself staring into a pair of huge dark eyes. The baby let out a hungry cry, and the woman quickly held it to her breast to stop the loud noise it made in the quiet night. She gasped at the touch of the small mouth against her skin, and sat down suddenly on the riverbank, among the reeds at the edge of the waters. After a few minutes she put the child down. Her fingers worked quickly, tearing the reeds and making them into a basket, just the right size for a new-born baby. She sent up a prayer to the gods, as she placed her daughter in the basket and pushed it into the gentle waters. She watched until the basket was out of sight. When the first fingers of the sun stroked the earth, river, and trees to light, the woman stood up and began the long walk back.

She placed her daughter in the basket and pushed it into the gentle waters.

Family

CATHERINE LIM

A story from Singapore, retold by Clare West

*'Money makes the world go around' is the title
of a song; another song is just called 'Money
Money Money'. In one way or another, money
affects everyone's life, but as yet another famous
song title says, 'Money can't buy me love'.*

*When an elderly parent dies, it is a sad time
for a family. The children come to mourn the
dead, and to remember the happy moments of
the past. Money, of course, is the last thing on
their minds . . .*

What should they do about the Old Biscuit Tin?

It was no piece of rubbish; its precious contents
earned it an almost religious respect from the family, and in
its presence their quarrelling was reduced to near silence. It
was a Jacob's Cream Crackers tin, and when they saw the
faded green picture of Jacob, the man who started the Cream
Crackers company, their loud voices quietened to a grateful
whisper. Their restless fingers felt the outline of his kind,
fatherly face on the tin – this was the face which had guarded
the treasure all these years.

But earlier, when they were clearing out the enormous pile
of old biscuit and cigarette tins, boxes and paper bags full of
nameless, useless things from under Old Mother's bed, they had

not the slightest idea. They carried huge armfuls of the rubbish out of the house and into the backyard, made a great fire and put an end to a lifetime's habit of saving, all the while shaking their heads in smiling disbelief. It was understood among adult children that an old parent must have a safe, peaceful home, but Old Mother had made her house into a death-trap.

'Your prayer candles could easily have set fire to all this rubbish and you could have died in your bed.'

'You could have cut yourself on one of those nasty tins and died of a terrible illness, living alone like this. You know that, don't you, Mother?'

The Old One, sitting on her bed, came out of her long silence to demand the return of the chocolate tin with the damaged lid.

'Bring it back. I want it back.'

After much patient questioning, it became clear that the chocolate tin with the damaged lid contained a precious load: the six umbilical cords, saved from the births of the six sons and daughters over forty years, each tied with yellow thread and wrapped in lucky red paper. Mothers usually presented these to their children when they were grown up, to remind them of childhood and a mother's love. But Old Mother had kept silent through the years. In the silence of her loneliness, each cord had seemed to be laughing at her.

'I want all of them back.'

It was too late to save the umbilical cords. The family searched through the burning rubbish, muttering their annoyance, but could not find them.

'Why didn't she tell us before we cleared it all out? She's being difficult, as always!'

'No harm done. Nobody would want to keep those things.'

There were other things the Old One asked for, and the family were forced to make more fruitless searches in the burning ruins of lost memories.

Then she said firmly, 'I want the Jacob's Cream Crackers tin back. Bring it back at once.'

'There are hundreds of these old tins! Which one?'

'The one tied with string. I want it back.'

'Why didn't you tell us before? And what is so special about this tin that you want it back?'

'I keep all my jewels in it,' said the Old One, 'in a red cloth bundle.'

It was a desperate search; sons and daughters, shouting for help to their sons and daughters, rushed out of the house all together in a group. They put sticks and bare hands into the fire, gasping and coughing in the heat and smoke. Standing at some distance, Eldest Son organized the search. At last someone pulled out a completely blackened tin, heavy with promise. The cover fell open instantly, and the jewels spilled out like a river, flashing with colour and light.

'Quick, pick up everything, put them back into the tin, and get back into the house. Make sure nothing is left behind!' ordered Eldest Son, fearful that neighbours were watching.

Their joy and relief over the recovered treasure took away the hard edges in their voices as they gathered to give advice to their foolish mother. She hid her money in rice bags and vegetable boxes and then forgot all about it, talked for hours to her dead husband's photograph, and, hoping to gain a place in heaven, gave their hard-earned money to the greedy monks who lived nearby.

'Mother, why don't you let us put the jewels in the bank for you?'

'Mother, why don't you let us employ you a servant?'

'Mother, why don't you let us remove you from this awful place of nasty neighbours and cheating monks?'

'Mother—'

'I'm a useless old woman who is not fit to live with her sons and daughters! So leave me alone!'

It was always like that. They would urge safety, convenience, pure common sense, but she simply refused to listen – she thought she knew best.

'Last week,' said Eldest Son's wife, using that special, gentle voice that people use for an awkward old person who won't listen, 'a burglar broke into old Ah Por's flat and stole all her gold chains. She thought they were safe, because she had hidden them, wrapped in some old clothes, in an old shoe-box on the top shelf of her cupboard, but the burglar knew.'

'Leave me alone!'

The Old One crossly took back the Old Biscuit Tin, got up and carried it to a cupboard where she pushed it roughly into a pile of clothes. She locked the cupboard with a key from a bunch at her waist. Then she sat down, and the tightness around her mouth told them they should go and leave her alone now. The loneliness of aloneness was more bearable than having them all there.

'Mother, take care.'

'Call if you need anything.'

'Don't let anyone know about the Old Biscuit Tin.'

When they were gone, she put her hands to her head, and rocked from side to side, crying softly in her misery. Then she lit a candle in front of her dead husband's photo and prayed silently to him.

They continued to refer to it as the Old Biscuit Tin, as if it were empty and worthless. They avoided mentioning its true value, in case that might make it disappear in some way. But in their deepest, most private thoughts, they saw again and again the spilling jewels – shining brooches, rings, bracelets, earrings, chains, hairpins, and necklaces falling in slow motion, each outlined in the firelight before it touched the ground and lay temptingly there. The memory of this wonderful treasure saved just in time from destructive flames and thieving neighbours gave them a stronger feeling of brave and selfless rescue than if they had saved a hundred men, women, and children from a terrible death.

Now the treasure lay undisturbed in the Old One's cupboard, along with the cheap little pieces of jewellery that they gave her regularly for her birthdays or the Chinese New Year. Second Son's wife said she had managed to catch sight of the slim gold bracelet she had given Old Mother on her sixty-fifth birthday. Third Daughter said that the small jade ring she had given was pitiable beside the richness of the jade necklace that Old Mother had inherited from her own mother. Both agreed that Old Mother was the luckiest woman in the world – she had treasure coming both ways, downwards from her own mother and upwards from her children. Both complained that they would never own jewellery to match a tiny part of Old Mother's wonderful collection, and wondered when was the last time Old Mother wore those huge diamonds and jade pieces.

⟫≫⊰⊰

Dutiful sons and daughters were allowed to joke playfully about an old parent's wealth, but not to make any serious attempt to count up that tempting wealth as long as the old parent was alive. Now she was dying, so it was proper to ask: what should they do about the Old Biscuit Tin?

She was dying, and she had left no instructions. Upstairs, a monk was singing prayers to assist the peaceful passing of Old Mother's soul. Downstairs, Eldest Son gathered the family to make the important decision about the Old Biscuit Tin.

'Sell the jewels and use the money for the funeral expenses, which are going to be very, very heavy. There's the large fee to pay those monks for the four nights of prayers that Old Mother has requested.'

'No, the jewels should not be sold. They are too rare and valuable. Anyway, they have emotional value.'

'Who cares about emotional value nowadays?'

'It's crazy for the dead to leave the living with a mountain of debt!' Third Son seldom spoke, and was soon told by his wife to be quiet.

'Share the jewels equally.'

'How is that to be done? And will that include grandchildren?' It was obvious why Second Son's wife said this; she had the largest number of children.

'No, wait, I've got an idea.' Eldest Son's wife became very excited. 'Let's have a two-step plan. Step one, separate the jewels into those given to Old Mother by us over the years, and those which are her own. We each take back what we have given. Step two, divide the rest equally, each of us choosing what he or she wants, taking turns, until it's all finished. The remaining odd ones go to Second Daughter.'

Second Daughter was the least wealthy of the six sons and daughters, as her husband was a lazy man, who gambled and wasted his time and money.

'Who has first choice?'

They were all thinking of the *krongsang*, a wonderful row of three hand-sized diamond brooches connected by a thick gold chain; whoever had the *krongsang* had the prize.

'Eldest first, but I am prepared to give up my place,' said First Daughter, conscious of her selfless generosity.

'Sons first, daughters next.'

'Who says sons must come before daughters?'

For the first time, a voice was unsuitably raised in a house of death; it was met by the gentle sound of the monk's prayers floating downstairs, and it was lowered. All voices were reduced to deep silence by a loud cry from Old Mother, coming up from the depths of her sad loneliness.

The silence was broken by someone saying, 'Ask Old Mother. Ask her what her wishes are about the Old Biscuit Tin.'

A deeper silence followed, heavy with fearful thoughts. What if the old woman, as a last foolish desire, demanded to be buried with the jewels? Once, a very old woman had insisted on being buried with a pair of extremely valuable jade bracelets.

But no dutiful child had ever refused an old parent's dying wish. So the sons and daughters concentrated on finding the best time to ask Old Mother the all-important question.

'It had better be now. Old Mother will die before sunrise.' And Second Daughter's eyes filled with tears at Old Mother's brave determination to die before the first light of day, before any of the day's meals were eaten – it was her way of saying to her children, 'I go without food so that you may have plenty!' They would show how much they appreciated this sacrifice on the day of the Feast of the Hungry Ghosts, when they would pile the most delicious food on Old Mother's grave for her ghost to eat. Meanwhile, they needed to know her wish about the Old Biscuit Tin.

The six sons and daughters went up the stairs as the monk came smoothly down. They nodded their heads in greeting, and said, 'Thank you, Reverend,' but only out of politeness. Eldest Son, as the head of the family, had the responsibility of asking Old Mother the question. She lay very still, looking pale and making soft little noises in her throat, like the low cries of a bird.

'What would you like us to do about the Old Biscuit Tin, Mother?' he asked.

She did not seem to understand. The others came closer, describing its rescue from the flames. They bent over her. Her bunch of keys lay on the bedside table; they pointed to it.

'Old Biscuit Tin,' they repeated urgently, 'with all your jewels and ours inside.'

Old Mother's eyes flew open for a second. She tried to lift a weak finger, and out of her mouth, with huge effort, came one name: 'The Reverend!'

Then she was gone. It was just past midnight.

Postponed anger is all the greater; outside the death room, the sons and daughters looked at one another in shocked silence.

'We can't simply hand over the Old Biscuit Tin to that monk!'

'Mother must have lost her mind.'

'That monk! What a hold he had on our mother—'

'She was probably giving money to the monks without our knowledge.'

'He'd been visiting her for years, even before her illness—'

'Stop giving people the wrong idea. Our mother was never as lonely or stupid as that.'

'I'm not giving people the wrong idea. I'm saying he's an extremely clever and greedy man, who was able to deceive her because she had such a trusting nature.'

'What would he do with the jewels?'

'What would he do, indeed? How can you ask such a stupid question? He'll sell them, of course, and use the money for religious purposes. He's been waiting for this to happen, pretending all the time to be offering prayers for her soul.'

The voices remained quiet in respect for the person who had so recently died, but their anger at the unfairness of it all was rising dangerously. It was fully directed at the evil monk who intended to steal their rightful inheritance from under their noses.

Eldest Son said, 'As head of the family, I make the decision to ignore the last wish of a parent who had clearly lost her mind. I make the decision to divide the Old Biscuit Tin into six equal shares, for each of the six sons and daughters. Grandchildren will not be included.'

'What about the ways of dividing it up? We went through this before. How—'

But the doubter was silenced by the sharpest remark so far from First Daughter: 'For goodness' sake, let's be civilized and not quarrel about how to share! Let's get out the Old Biscuit Tin quickly and put an end to the matter once and for all. This has been a most upsetting day!'

Eldest Son, being head of the family, fetched the key. He opened the cupboard and brought out the Old Biscuit Tin, frowning. He frowned still more when he put the tin on the table in full view of the others, lifted the cover easily and said angrily, 'I thought so. It felt too light.' The Old Biscuit Tin was empty except for a cheap gold ring and a pair of small earrings lying miserably inside on the red cloth.

'They're gone, all gone!'

First Daughter ran her hand desperately all over the inside of

The Old Biscuit Tin was empty except for a cheap gold ring and a pair of small earrings.

the old rusty tin, as if to feel for a secret place where the jewels might have hidden themselves.

'Oh do be careful!' cried Second Daughter, as First Daughter pulled up her hand with a sharp cry and started licking the blood off a small cut near her wrist.

Blood, tears, loss, betrayal – all were blamed on the monk.

'He's stolen all the jewels!' gasped Eldest Son's wife. 'He took all the jewels from the Old Biscuit Tin and left these two miserable bits.' She held up the almost worthless ring and earrings in shocked disbelief.

The monk's wickedness grew with every cry of loss. They had already felt the deepest hatred for him, because he was the person intended to inherit the family treasure. Now that he actually possessed it, their most urgent wish was to show him how furious they were, face to face.

'Get him now! Quick, somebody, go and find him and bring him here.'

'Force him to return the jewels.'

'Suppose he's already sold them?'

'Then get the police!'

Eldest Son shouted, 'Quiet, all of you! We have to use our brains in these dangerous times, and here are all of you crying and talking nonsense. Of course he didn't steal the jewels. He's much too clever for that. He worked his power on a poor ignorant lonely old woman and made her give them to him – a totally legal gift to the monks. There is no crime, don't bring the police in.'

'What are we to do?' whispered First Daughter in a trembling voice. She was feeling very ill.

'Legal action,' said Eldest Son. 'We shall have to think carefully and move fast.'

Meanwhile, the rules of correct behaviour required all activities to stop, in order to allow the proper funeral arrangements to be made. Eldest Son and his wife were in charge, giving instructions. At the funeral the rest were there, shoulder to shoulder, giving the impression of a family working solidly together at a time of great suffering. A dutiful son or daughter was permitted no unkind thought towards a dead parent. So Old Mother, laid out in her funeral clothes and attended by three praying monks, was surrounded by her entire family, all in black mourning clothes and with sad mourning faces.

She had died just after midnight, and that was very good, said the neighbours and visitors as they began coming to make their funeral visits – it showed what a very thoughtful parent she was, leaving all the good things of life for her children and grandchildren. A dutiful son or daughter was permitted one small thought, as long as it remained unspoken for the moment: it would have been better if she had saved herself the trouble of dying at that time and left the Old Biscuit Tin instead.

The Old Biscuit Tin, lying on its side on the floor, with the insulting gold ring and cheap earrings still inside, was stuck between the leg of a chair and the wall, where Eldest Son had kicked it in a burst of uncontrollable anger. A picture of it rose in Eldest Son's mind during the funeral ceremony as he sat on the floor with his legs crossed beside Old Mother's body, surrounded by the other mourners. The thought of the Old Biscuit Tin re-awoke his anger, changing the expression on his face to one of poisonous hatred that was hardly suitable for a house of mourning.

The Reverend came in, wearing yellow, and started to

murmur his prayers over Old Mother's still peaceful body. At the same time, as part of the ceremony, he rang a small bell.

The dead woman, the praying monk, the empty Old Biscuit Tin – these three things together added up to the worst kind of evil, a wicked trick that had deceived sons, daughters, and grandchildren. Eldest Son was leading the rest of the family in procession round Old Mother's body, when suddenly, for him, the last chains enforcing a son's or daughter's duties broke. He was able, right in the middle of the ceremony, to plan the first step of the legal action they would take to get their revenge.

In his mind he started writing the statement he was going to give the lawyers. *She was a lonely, simple, trusting old woman with odd habits,* the statement would begin. *And in her loneliness she behaved strangely, which upset her sons and daughters very much, because her actions were against her own safety and against the interests of her family . . .*

GLOSSARY

ancestor   a person in your family who lived a long time ago

ash   the grey powder that is left after a cigarette has burnt

battery   an electrical device, placed inside a toy, clock, watch, etc.

biscuit   a flat, thin, dry cake

blouse   a piece of clothing like a shirt, worn by women

blush   to become red in the face, especially when embarrassed

breasts   the two soft round parts at the front of a woman's body

brooch   a piece of jewellery which can be pinned to your clothes

bum *(informal)*   the part of the body that you sit on

catalogue   an illustrated booklet showing goods for sale

charioteer   the driver of a chariot (a vehicle pulled by horses);
     in the *Bhagavad Gita*, a famous Hindu poem, Lord Krishna
     becomes 'the beloved charioteer' of the warrior prince, Arjuna,
     and gives him practical and spiritual advice before battle

cheek   the side of the face below the eye

chicken-feed company *(informal)*   a company which is not large
     enough to be important, and which people will ignore

coincidence   two things happening at the same time by chance

Cream Crackers   very dry biscuits

elder, eldest   older/oldest (used of members of a family)

exile   having to live away from your own country

groom   short for bridegroom, a man on his wedding day

guy *(informal)*   a man

harmony   a state of peaceful existence and agreement;
     harmonious *(adj)*   friendly, peaceful; musically very pleasant

hut   a very small building or shelter, often made of wood

jade   a hard green stone used in making jewellery and ornaments

kiln   *(here)* an oven in which bricks are made

lantern   *(here)* a lamp inside a paper case, with a handle to carry it

mat   *(here)* a piece of thick cloth on the floor, for sleeping on

Mickey Mouse   a character from Walt Disney cartoon films

missionary   a person sent abroad to teach people about religion

monk   a member of a religious group of men who do not marry

mooncake   a Chinese cake traditionally eaten during the Mid-
Autumn Festival

mourn   to feel and show sadness because someone has died

mutter   to speak in a low voice that is hard to hear

nail   a thin hard layer covering the outer tip of the finger

olive   a small green or black fruit with a strong taste

Ovaltine   a hot milky drink

panties   a piece of women's underwear that covers the body
from the waist to the tops of the legs

peasant   someone who baves badly, or has little education

pee *(v)*   to pass waste liquid from your body

Planter's Punch and Singapore Sling   alcoholic drinks often drunk
by Europeans who once controlled some Asian countries

pole   a long, thin, straight piece of wood

primary school   *(in Singapore)* a school for children aged 7 to 11

pyjamas   loose trousers and a loose shirt, worn to sleep in

radiogram   a radio and a record player combined in one box

Red Guards   students and workers in the Cultural Revolution
(1966–1976) who were encouraged by the Chinese leader Mao
Tse Tung to attack people who disagreed with his ideas

Reverend   *(here)* a way of speaking to a monk; **the Reverend** a
way of speaking about a monk

sari   a kind of dress worn by women in South Asia

secondary school *(in Singapore)*   a school for pupils aged 11 to 16

sedan   a box containing seating for two people, carried on poles,
used as part of a traditional wedding ceremony in China

slave a person who has to work very hard for someone

snore to breathe noisily through your mouth while you are asleep

sock a piece of clothing worn over the foot

spices different powders or seeds from plants, which are used in cooking, e.g. **chilli, pepper, fenugrefi, cardamom**

sweat liquid that appears on the skin when you are hot

Tamil a member of a race of people living in Tamil Nadu in southern India and in Sri Lanka; the language of the Tamils

teddy bear a soft toy animal in the shape of a bear

trade *(v)* to buy and sell things; **trading** *(n)* the activity of buying and selling things

treasure a collection of valuable things, e.g. gold, silver, jewels

trumpet a brass musical instrument made of a curved metal tube

umbilical cord a long piece of flesh which connects a baby to its mother's body, and which is cut at the moment of birth

veiled wearing a piece of thin material over the face

verandah a platform with an open front and roof, built on the side of a house on the ground floor

yuan the unit of money in China

NON-ENGLISH WORDS USED IN THESE STORIES

ajji grandmother

Amma mother

Appa father

gfi sim very unhappy

Hanh? used when asking a question

Suernai a trumpet used to make music in a wedding ceremony

ACTIVITIES

Before Reading

Before you read each story, read the introduction on the first page. Then use the questions below to help you make some guesses about each story.

1 *Taken for a Ride* (story introduction page 1). Who do you think Jinnan finds in the wedding sedan chair this time?

2 *The First Party* (story introduction page 9). Why doesn't the young wife enjoy her first party?

3 *Fair Trade* (story introduction page 16). How will the fashion models change the islanders' lives?

4 *Mid-Autumn* (story introduction page 36). Why did the daughter move away from her family to another country?

5 *Anil* (story introduction page 47). What do you think happens on that hot March night in Anil's village?

6 *My Beloved Charioteer* (story introduction page 57). Why is there tension between the grandmother and her daughter Aarti?

7 *A Dream of China* (story introduction page 68). Why does the daughter's return to China turn out to be disappointing?

8 *Lily* (story introduction page 82). Why do you think Adam's marriage broke down?

9 *A Child is Born* (story introduction page 89). What do you think will happen if the baby is a girl?

10 *Family* (story introduction page 92). What are the dying person's children really interested in?

ACTIVITIES

After Reading

1 **Read these quotations from some of the stories. Then think about the questions that follow and give your opinions.**

1 This was probably his son's only chance of escape from a life with no hope. *Anil* (page 55, lines 28/29)
   Was Ragunathan right to accept the headman's offer and send Anil away to the city?

2 Not surprisingly, Lisa got a divorce and was allowed to keep Lily. *Lily* (page 86, lines 17/18)
   Was Lisa justified in making it difficult for Adam to see his daughter, or was she punishing him too cruelly?

3 Her discomfort changed to anger, and she stared at the strange creatures around her. *The First Party* (page 11, lines 14/15)
   What advice would you give to the young wife in this story?

4 We can never escape the responsibility of being parents. *My Beloved Charioteer* (page 63, lines 5/6)
   Was the grandmother right to blame herself for Aarti's bitterness?

5 'My boyfriend just wanted to have some fun.' *Taken for a Ride* (page 8, lines 11/12)
   Do you think Lili made the right decisions in her life?

6 Out of her mouth, with huge effort, came one name: 'The Reverend!' *Family* (page 99, lines 14/15)
   Was Old Mother right to give all the family jewels away to the monks?

7 Girls, she had been told since childhood, brought only tears and unhappiness to others. *A Child is Born* (page 90, lines 14/15)
   What can be done to prevent this kind of tragedy occurring?

2 Here are the thoughts of ten characters (one from each story).
   Which stories are they from, who is thinking, and what has just
   happened?

   1 'Giving me orders all the time! Do this, do that! They pretend
      they are concerned about me, but I know there's only one thing
      they want. Well, I won't let them have it – it's safely locked
      away now. Oh, I'm so alone, so alone – it's miserable being
      old.'

   2 'Look at those long, long legs, man! Just like the girls in
      Murali's magazines. That one, maybe I can make her smile a
      bit. But I'd better keep sweeping – the boss might come out any
      minute . . .'

   3 'That's him singing to us. I feel so ashamed. He was a good
      man, but the smell of his feet! And the snoring! No, marriage is
      not for me. I want to stay young, not grow old with him.'

   4 'What a relief! The boy's on that train, and he won't be coming
      back in a hurry. The villagers will stop talking about my wife's
      death very soon. Now no one can prove that I used to beat her
      every night – my secret's safe.'

   5 'I think I said the wrong thing when Mummy asked me. I do
      remember Father, but only just. Mummy looked so angry – it
      made me very sad. In the old photos she looks very happy. But
      I've never seen her like that . . .'

   6 'Self, self, self – he's just thinking of his own problems as usual!
      Why does he go on and on about his wife and child? What
      about *me*? Don't I deserve a bit of attention? If he isn't careful,
      I might say no next time he wants to come round for the night!'

   7 'That's no good. It's a son that we need, not a daughter. We can't
      even pay the midwife. Well, there's nothing we can do now. She
      must get rid of it as quickly as possible. If not, I will.'

8 'Silly girl, sitting there with that disapproving look on her face. I can't believe she refused to dance with me! So embarrassing, in front of my friends. I should never have brought her. Well, she's had her chance – she'll stay at home next time . . .'

9 'Has she baked a mooncake for me, I wonder? Oh, my hands are so painful! I don't know how much more of this work I can take. But do I want to go home and live in comfort? No, I really think God is telling me to stay . . .'

10 'What's the use of having family in Singapore if they won't even help me get out? And look what she's left me with – a camera with one roll of film! And no cigarettes! It's not as if they ever send much money – they keep their wealth to themselves!'

3 **Imagine that these letters were written by characters in the stories. Use the notes below to help you write the letters.**

1 In *Fair Trade*, after the models leave, Manju writes to Alice:
   • She asks how Alice is, and gives her some news of the island.
   • She asks if Alice would very kindly send the ring back.
   • She explains the importance of the ring to her family.

2 In *Mid-Autumn*, a friend of the mother's writes to the daughter in Africa:
   • She explains how depressed and sad her mother is.
   • She says it is a daughter's duty to help her parents.
   • She asks the daughter to come home for her mother's sake.

3 In *A Dream of China*, the daughter writes to her father, just before her return:
   • She describes the beautiful things she has seen in China.
   • She says that his brother and wife are well.
   • She gives the impression that it has been a successful visit.

4 Which story did you like best in this book? Write three or four
   sentences to explain why. Use some of these words to help you.

setting	dialogue	storyline
atmosphere	humour	ending
descriptions	pathos	message
characters		

5 Here is a short poem (a kind of poem called a haiku) about one of
   the stories. Which of the ten stories is it about?

   > *Hanging from a tree*
   > *A woman is a victim*
   > *But a small boy knows.*

   Here is another haiku. Which story is this one about?

   > *Who should inherit?*
   > *The quarrelling family*
   > *Or the men of God?*

   A haiku is a Japanese poem, which is always in three lines, and the
   three lines always have 5, 7 and 5 syllables each, like this:

   | Hang | ing | from | a | tree | = 5 syllables
   | A | wo | man | is | a | vic | tim | = 7 syllables
   | But | a | small | boy | knows | = 5 syllables

   Now write your own haiku, one for each of the other eight stories.
   Think about what each story is really about. What are the important
   ideas for you? Remember to keep to three lines of 5, 7, 5 syllables
   each.

ABOUT THE AUTHORS

LIU HONG

Liu Hong (1965–) was born in Manchuria, North East China. After studying English Literature at university, she worked as a teacher and translator in Beijing. She came to live in England in 1989, and has written four novels: *Startling Moon*, *The Magpie Bridge*, *The Touch*, and *Wives of the East Wind*. Her short story, *Taken for a Ride*, was commissioned and broadcast by BBC Radio 4 in 2008. She says, 'At my wedding in China, we hired a sedan chair and the man who guided the chair had the most beaming smile. My husband and I were intrigued by this man. What if there were some sadness b›ind his smile? Hence the story.'

ATTIA HOSAIN

Attia Hosain (1913–1998) was born in Lucknow, Northern India, and grew up knowing many of the political and literary figures of the time. She starting writing short stories while at college: 'I always wanted to write and (an idea) would go round and round in my head and sometimes I would put it down and sometimes I wouldn't.' She came to England after the partition of India in 1947, and published a collection of short stories, *Phoenix Fled* (1953), and a novel, *Sunlight on a Broken Column* (1961). For many years she was a BBC Urdu programme presenter to India and Pakistan, and had a successful career in the theatre and other media.

PREETA SAMARASAN

Preeta Samarasan was born in Malaysia and moved to the USA to finish her education. She gained her MFA in creative writing from the University of Michigan. Her novel, *Evening is the Whole Day* (2008), was shortlisted for the Commonwealth Prize for Best First Book. Her story *Fair Trade* was inspired by a catalogue from a popular American clothing company who did a photo shoot in Sri Lanka. Although the plot is invented and the setting has been changed, the story retains the author's shocked reaction to the colonialist overtones of the original photographs. She now lives with her husband and daughter in a village in central France.

HWEE HWEE TAN

Hwee Hwee Tan (1974–) was born in Singapore. She has lived in the Netherlands and in England, where she studied English at the universities of East Anglia and Oxford. She has won awards for her short stories, and her first novel, *Foreign Bodies*, was published in 1997. She studied creative writing at New York University, and her second novel, *Mammon Inc* (2001), won the 2004 Singapore Literature Prize. She says about writing, 'I think the key is knowing what is unique about your country and about your place.' She now lives in Singapore.

RIDJAL NOOR

Ridjal Noor (1979–) was born in Singapore, the descendant of Indian grandparents who had migrated to Singapore when it was newly independent. He has a degree in Communications and Media Management, and runs a design studio and a printing company in Singapore. He started writing when he was seventeen, and in his stories he explores the Indian way of life, delving into his forefathers' history and culture. His writing has been published in Malaysia, Australia, and the United Kingdom.

SHASHI DESHPANDE

Shashi Deshpande, who lives in Bangalore, India, has written a large number of short stories, ten novels, many essays, and done some translations. Her most recent novel, *In the Country of Deceit*, was shortlisted for the Regional Commonwealth Writers' Prize, 2009. Her stories and novels have been translated into various Indian and European languages. The inspiration for *My Beloved Charioteer* came to her, she remembers, from watching a sentimental Hindi movie about mourning the death of a loved one. She says writing was never a conscious decision for her. 'It was something which was waiting for me along the line, . . . and then I knew what my life was going to be about.'

OVIDIA YU

Ovidia Yu (1961–) was born in, lives in, and writes about Singapore and Singapore people. As well as short stories, she has had two novels published and over thirty plays performed, for which she has received several awards. *A Dream of China* was written for a short story competition. 'I write all the time. Writing about people and situations is how I understand them – or try to,' she says. An unusual source of inspiration for her stories is her shopping trips, where she walks around shopping centres and eavesdrops on conversations, taking notes wherever she goes.

NORA ADAM

Noraishah Ismail (who writes under the name Nora Adam) was born in Malaysia, and lives and works in Kuala Lumpur. She had always wanted to be a writer, but her parents insisted she chose a 'proper' profession, so she started work as a lawyer in 1999, writing stories in her spare time. She finds that the best time for creating them is in the middle of the night when the whole house is quiet, her family is asleep, and she finally has the space to think and write. The idea for *Lily* came from a gossip session with a few old friends about infidelity; one night soon afterwards she wrote the first draft from start to finish, until it was almost dawn.

NIRUPAMA SUBRAMANIAN

Nirupama Subramanian lives with her husband and daughter in Gurgaon, India. She has an MA in Business Management, and now works as a Human Resources consultant. She has written for publications in India and abroad, and her first novel, *Keep the Change*, was published in 2010. A passionate believer in the rights of the girl child, she does voluntary work for a shelter for homeless girls. *A Child is Born*, one of the winning stories in the 2006 Commonwealth Short Story competition, is a result of what she has seen and read about female infanticide, which is still prevalent in many parts of India. She hopes more people will cherish and treasure their daughters in the future.

CATHERINE LIM

Catherine Lim (1942–) was born in Malaysia (then Malaya), and is now a writer and political commentator in Singapore. She has a PhD in Applied Linguistics, and lectured in Sociolinguistics and Literature before becoming a full-time writer. Her first novel, *The Serpent's Tooth*, came out in 1982. She has published eighteen books, including short stories, novels, and a book of poems, and has received many awards. Her major theme is the role of women in traditional Chinese society and culture. She says, 'I would like to see myself as a keen, perceptive and, above all, caring chronicler of the human condition.'

OXFORD BOOKWORMS LIBRARY

Classics • Crime & Mystery • Factfiles • Fantasy & Horror
Human Interest • Playscripts • Thriller & Adventure
True Stories • World Stories

The OXFORD BOOKWORMS LIBRARY provides enjoyable reading in English, with a wide range of classic and modern fiction, non-fiction, and plays. It includes original and adapted texts in seven carefully graded language stages, which take learners from beginner to advanced level. An overview is given on the next pages.

All Stage 1 titles are available as audio recordings, as well as over eighty other titles from Starter to Stage 6. All Starters and many titles at Stages 1 to 4 are specially recommended for younger learners. Every Bookworm is illustrated, and Starters and Factfiles have full-colour illustrations.

The OXFORD BOOKWORMS LIBRARY also offers extensive support. Each book contains an introduction to the story, notes about the author, a glossary, and activities. Additional resources include tests and worksheets, and answers for these and for the activities in the books. There is advice on running a class library, using audio recordings, and the many ways of using Oxford Bookworms in reading programmes. Resource materials are available on the website <www.oup.com/bookworms>.

The *Oxford Bookworms Collection* is a series for advanced learners. It consists of volumes of short stories by well-known authors, both classic and modern. Texts are not abridged or adapted in any way, but carefully selected to be accessible to the advanced student.

You can find details and a full list of titles in the *Oxford Bookworms Library Catalogue* and *Oxford English Language Teaching Catalogues*, and on the website <www.oup.com/bookworms>.

THE OXFORD BOOKWORMS LIBRARY
GRADING AND SAMPLE EXTRACTS

STARTER • 250 HEADWORDS

present simple – present continuous – imperative –
can/cannot, must – *going to* (future) – simple gerunds ...

Her phone is ringing – but where is it?

Sally gets out of bed and looks in her bag. No phone. She looks under the bed. No phone. Then she looks behind the door. There is her phone. Sally picks up her phone and answers it. *Sally's Phone*

STAGE 1 • 400 HEADWORDS

... past simple – coordination with *and*, *but*, *or* –
subordination with *before*, *after*, *when*, *because*, *so* ...

I knew him in Persia. He was a famous builder and I worked with him there. For a time I was his friend, but not for long. When he came to Paris, I came after him – I wanted to watch him. He was a very clever, very dangerous man. *The Phantom of the Opera*

STAGE 2 • 700 HEADWORDS

... present perfect – *will* (future) – *(don't)* have to, *must not, could* –
comparison of adjectives – simple *if* clauses – past continuous –
tag questions – *ask/tell* + infinitive ...

While I was writing these words in my diary, I decided what to do. I must try to escape. I shall try to get down the wall outside. The window is high above the ground, but I have to try. I shall take some of the gold with me – if I escape, perhaps it will be helpful later. *Dracula*

STAGE 3 • 1000 HEADWORDS

... should, may – present perfect continuous – *used to* – past perfect –
causative – relative clauses – indirect statements ...

Of course, it was most important that no one should see
Colin, Mary, or Dickon entering the secret garden. So Colin
gave orders to the gardeners that they must all keep away
from that part of the garden in future. *The Secret Garden*

STAGE 4 • 1400 HEADWORDS

*... past perfect continuous – passive (simple forms) –
would* conditional clauses – indirect questions –
relatives with *where/when* – gerunds after prepositions/phrases ...

I was glad. Now Hyde could not show his face to the world
again. If he did, every honest man in London would be
proud to report him to the police. *Dr Jekyll and Mr Hyde*

STAGE 5 • 1800 HEADWORDS

*... future continuous – future perfect –
passive (modals, continuous forms) –
would have* conditional clauses – modals + perfect infinitive ...

If he had spoken Estella's name, I would have hit him. I was
so angry with him, and so depressed about my future, that I
could not eat the breakfast. Instead I went straight to the old
house. *Great Expectations*

STAGE 6 • 2500 HEADWORDS

... passive (infinitives, gerunds) – advanced modal meanings –
clauses of concession, condition

When I stepped up to the piano, I was confident. It was as if
I knew that the prodigy side of me really did exist. And when I
started to play, I was so caught up in how lovely I looked that I
didn't worry how I would sound. *The Joy Luck Club*

WORLD STORIES FROM BOOKWORMS

The Meaning of Gifts: Stories from Turkey
STAGE 1   RETOLD BY JENNIFER BASSETT

Cries from the Heart: Stories from Around the World *
STAGE 2   RETOLD BY JENNIFER BASSETT

Changing their Skies: Stories from Africa
STAGE 2   RETOLD BY JENNIFER BASSETT

Songs from the Soul: Stories from Around the World
STAGE 2   RETOLD BY JENNIFER BASSETT

The Long White Cloud: Stories from New Zealand
STAGE 3   RETOLD BY CHRISTINE LINDOP

Dancing with Strangers: Stories from Africa *
STAGE 3   RETOLD BY CLARE WEST

Playing with Fire: Stories from the Pacific Rim *
STAGE 3   RETOLD BY JENNIFER BASSETT

Leaving No Footprint: Stories from Asia
STAGE 3   RETOLD BY CLARE WEST

A Cup of Kindness: Stories from Scotland
STAGE 3   RETOLD BY JENNIFER BASSETT

Doors to a Wider Place: Stories from Australia
STAGE 4   RETOLD BY CHRISTINE LINDOP

Land of my Childhood: Stories from South Asia **
STAGE 4   RETOLD BY CLARE WEST

The Price of Peace: Stories from Africa
STAGE 4   RETOLD BY CHRISTINE LINDOP

Treading on Dreams: Stories from Ireland
STAGE 5   RETOLD BY CLARE WEST

Gazing at Stars: Stories from Asia
STAGE 6   RETOLD BY CLARE WEST

** Winner: Language Learner Literature Awards
* Finalist: Language Learner Literature Awards